PRAISE FOR *26 MARATHONS*

"*26 Marathons* gives great insight about the ups and downs of marathon running and how to cope with them. As Meb shows, dealing with these marathon experiences helps us become better in our lives."
—Eliud Kipchoge, marathon world record holder and 2016 Olympic gold medalist

"Meb's *26 Marathons* is like opening a treasure chest full of inspiring stories which give behind-the-scenes glimpses into the mental and physical joys and obstacles that elite-level racing can bring. His advice on training and overcoming injuries and adversity is for everyone. It's pure gold!"
—Shalane Flanagan, 2017 TCS NYC Marathon champion

"*26 Marathons* is a fantastic book. It's about setting goals and pursuing them, and about how to continue excelling in the midst of satisfactions and disappointments. Meb drives home the fact that winning in life isn't defined by coming in first place. This book is not just for runners. It will help you no matter what your passion in life might be."
—Tony Dungy, Super Bowl–winning coach, NFL Hall of Famer, and *New York Times* bestselling author

"Meb is as great a champion as I've ever known, and an even better person. *26 Marathons* is the perfect road map for your journey to the top of the mountain. This radiantly brilliant treatise on life through sports, family, faith, perseverance, and persistence epitomizes everything that I strive for on a path that Meb has already traveled. Thank you, Meb, for shining the light, for being the true giant among us, and for showing us that tomorrow is worth the effort to get there. Run on, beam on, teach on, carry on."

—Bill Walton, former NBA champion and MVP

"This book is a gift from Meb. I couldn't put it down as memories flooded back and his vivid descriptions put us in the races with him. Whether reading this one race at a time or by the years, first-timers and pros alike will be inspired to 'run to win' on and off the roads."

—Mary Wittenberg, former CEO of NY Road Runners and Virgin Sport

"I've watched Meb build a legendary career in distance running, one marathon at a time. *26 Marathons* is a captivating look at each race from his professional marathon career and the valuable lessons they taught him about running and life."

—John Legere, former CEO and president, T-Mobile

26
MARATHONS

What I Learned About Faith,
Identity, Running, *and* Life
from My Marathon Career

MEB KEFLEZIGHI
AND SCOTT DOUGLAS

RODALE.
NEW YORK

Originally published in hardcover in the United States by Rodale,
an imprint of Random House, a division of
Penguin Random House LLC, New York, in 2019.

For additional photo credits, see page 241.

Library of Congress Cataloging-in-Publication Data
is available upon request.

ISBN 978-0-593-13983-7
Ebook ISBN 978-1-63565-289-5

PRINTED IN THE UNITED STATES OF AMERICA

Book design by Andrea Lau
Jacket design by Pete Garceau
Jacket photograph by Alex Aristei

10 9 8 7 6 5 4 3 2

First Paperback Edition

To my parents, Russom and Awetash, who sacrificed their own lives to seek better opportunities for their children.

To Amoy Letemichael and Dr. Luigi Brindicci, who made a lot of the family journey possible. Without your big hearts, none of our successful results would have been possible. Rest in peace, Amoy.

To my brothers and sisters, who supported and understood my crazy schedule. I missed out on a lot, but now you know why.

To my wife, Yordanos, and our children, Sara, Fiyori, and Yohana. You are my inspiration.

To my classmates, teammates, teachers, coaches, and friends, and the people in the medical field who encouraged and challenged me to be my best in every aspect of life. Now these lessons are shared with others.

—Meb Keflezighi

CONTENTS

26 MARATHONS

INTRODUCTION

The first thing I see is the finish line behind me.

For a moment, I'm confused. Why am I lying on the ground with my head cradled in my hands? Then I remember: I've just finished the 2017 New York City Marathon and have collapsed in exhaustion.

In that moment I'm flooded by thoughts. I think about how I started my marathon career crossing this very finish line fifteen years earlier, and how after that first one I said I'd never run another. I think about changing my mind and trying the marathon again. I think about winning an Olympic silver medal in 2004, about a marathon in 2007 that almost ended my career, about coming back stronger than ever to win New York in 2009, about the bad marathons that almost caused me to quit the sport, about resolving to give it one more shot—and the redemption that came by winning Boston one year after the bombings there. It hits me that I've just completed my twenty-sixth marathon—one for each mile of the race, to end my professional running career.

For the first few seconds after finishing, I'm fine. Then I realize I'm shaking and am about to hit the ground hard. My instincts tell me to protect my head. I slump to the road like it's a bed, with my hands like a pillow. Then I'm unconscious.

When I come to, my main thought is to get up and let everyone know I'm okay. Before I can, my wife, Yordanos, our oldest daughter, Sara, and my good friend Dr. Andy Rosen come to the rescue. They and others try to lift me. I've never felt so heavy in my entire life. Once I'm on my feet I see our other daughters, Yohana and Fiyori, and my parents. People take turns keeping me stable. Pretty soon we find my brother and manager, Hawi, and my longtime coach and mentor, Bob Larsen. As I stagger around, the team that unceasingly supported me throughout my marathon career is now doing so literally. I think about how the marathon really is a metaphor for life. I've given my all, today and over the course of twenty-six marathons.

LESSONS LEARNED

Emil Zatopek, the only runner to win the 5K, 10K, and marathon in the same Olympics, said, "If you want to run, run a mile. If you want to experience a different life, run a marathon."

Each of my twenty-six professional marathons was not just a race against the top runners in the world, but a learning experience. I emerged from all of my marathons a smarter runner, a better racer, and a wiser person. Every race had moments, challenges, and triumphs that made for a unique learning experience. My goal in this book is to share the key takeaways from each race and show how to make use of those lessons in your own running and life.

The book is organized by marathon, one per chapter, presented chronologically. The lessons cover everything that contributed to my success, which is to say pretty much everything imaginable—pacing and race tactics, family and faith, nutrition and training, mental toughness and goal setting. I hope you'll feel like we're on a run together as I give an inside look at my marathon career and provide equal doses of inspiration and practical advice.

RUN TO WIN

The undercurrent running throughout this book is my "run to win" philosophy.

"Run to win" doesn't mean always trying to finish first. Even for elite runners, finishing first is the exception, not the rule. I broke the tape at only three of my twenty-six marathons. Sure, I hoped to and tried to win most of them, but when I placed something other than first, I was content as long as I had "run to win" in the broader sense.

What do I mean? Simply that "run to win" isn't about finishing first, but about getting the best out of yourself.

I started using this philosophy long before I became a marathoner. When I was a high school sophomore in San Diego, my Sunday routine started with church, followed by a trip to the house of Steve and Gail Van Camp. Their daughters, who were runners, were my academic tutors. They would help with my homework, especially English. Then I would mow the Van Camps' lawn, and I'd join the family for dinner, usually spaghetti. Over dinner Dr. and Mrs. Van Camp would ask me about my schoolwork and upcoming competitions. We would discuss my goals for the races. How fast did I think I could run? What would be a good showing? Did I think I could win? Who are the key contenders? It was homework on top of homework.

Thinking about my races that way helped me broaden my

definition of success. I realized that it could be just as satisfying to finish fifth instead of first if I could honestly say I'd given my best. Setting personal records took on new meaning, because they were indisputable evidence that I had done better than I ever had at a particular distance. With the Van Camps' help, I learned how to evaluate my performances in less-objective situations than a timed race on the track, including ones outside running.

This philosophy meshed well with Coach Larsen's approach once I got to UCLA and started working with him. As a college coach, Bob was overseeing the training and racing of dozens of athletes in different events. There's a great range of ages and abilities among college athletes; many people who were stars in high school struggle once they find themselves in the middle of the pack. Coach Larsen was great at getting everyone to think about what success would mean for them, regardless of how others performed. Being a UCLA Bruin also meant learning from legendary basketball coach John Wooden. He said, "Success is peace of mind, which is a direct result of self-satisfaction in knowing you made the effort to become the best of which you are capable."

I carried that mind-set into every marathon I ran. It was key to the many successes I had in my career, and it helped me through some very rough times. I hope that this book inspires you to "run to win" on your terms, in running and in life.

KEY LESSON

Marathoners always need to be grounded in reality.

don't want to do this ever again."

That's part of the entry from my running log for November 3, 2002, the day I ran my first marathon. The race was an inauspicious start to my marathon career. I knew that a lot of people say "Never again!" after marathons, but I was sincere. Running the last 10K at my easy run pace, despite great preparation and mental fortitude, was just utterly unsatisfying. I felt defeated by the distance.

Obviously, I didn't end up in the one-and-done club. Still, at one point in each of my twenty-six marathons as a pro I asked myself, "Why am I doing this?" (Yes, even when I won Boston.) I eventually learned that it's always going to hurt, but most of the time you can come out of that absolute pit. When you're conditioned properly and your body and mind are on the same page, it's a beautiful thing. Eventually I learned that the marathon can be the most satisfying event in running. It can even be fun.

I didn't have that experience the first time. When I hit the Wall after 20 miles, it was hard to override all of my negative thoughts. I like to say I got my PhD in marathoning that day. The theme of my dissertation: You need to base what you do on race day in reality, not fantasy.

A NEW CHALLENGE

I have always set ambitious goals. I thrive on accomplishing one difficult task and using it as a stepping-stone to another. That's how I came to be on the starting line of the New York City Marathon in 2002. I had started with the usual high school distance events of 1600 and 3200 meters (just short of 1 and 2 miles), moved up to the 5K and 10K in college, and started running longer road races after I became a pro in 1998. The marathon was the next logical step.

I had always been told my future was as a marathoner, even when, as a high school runner, my self-image was that I was a miler. One of my high school advisors, Ron Tabb, was a former elite marathoner who placed second at the 1983 Boston Marathon. He could see that my efficient running form, willingness to put up with a lot in training and racing, mental toughness, and tactical smarts would suit me well over 26.2 miles. After I set the American record for 10,000 meters in 2001, I wanted to see what the marathon was about. Coach Larsen, who had worked with many top marathoners, was excited about my potential.

Logistically, 2002 was a good time to debut. It was in the middle of an Olympic cycle and there were no track and field world championships, which are held every two years, in the years before and after the Olympics. Running New York would give me experience at the distance against a top international field on a challenging course. Plus, it's on everyone's bucket list to visit the Big Apple. That experience would give Coach Larsen and me insight on whether the marathon might be a good event for me to target for the 2004 Olympics. I would be twenty-seven on race day in New York, around the age that the conventional wisdom of the time said that distance runners are at their prime. (I'm proud to be among those who eventually proved that marathoners can thrive long after their late twenties.)

The switch from 10K training to marathon training wasn't a drastic change for me. I already did 20-mile runs on a regular basis, starting in college. I extended the distance of my long runs before New York, topping out with a 26- and a 27-miler so that I knew I could go the distance. Long runs of the marathon distance or farther became a regular part of my training for subsequent marathons when I was healthy and had the time to build up to them gradually. Doing runs that meant being on my feet for longer than I would be on race day helped me physically and psychologically. Overall, my training for New York was ideal, with a highest-mileage week of 125.

This was the first time I implemented practices that became standard throughout my marathon career. I monitored my weight. I tracked my heart rate on runs. I did a lot of self-care work and got a lot of professional physical treatment. All of these measures aimed to help me hold up to the stress of marathon training. When focusing on 10Ks, I had a few really hard days each week. Marathon training was more of a day-in-and-day-out grind, of steadily accumulating mileage and hard but not all-out workouts. I wanted to stay on top of my recovery so that I could absorb the training and not get injured.

Good recovery was especially important during my training in Mammoth Lakes, California, which sits at an altitude of just under 8,000 feet. It's easier to get run down at high elevations than at sea level, because your body is under extra stress from the limited oxygen. That's what makes altitude training effective— once you get accustomed physically and mentally to the more difficult conditions, racing at sea level is easier. For the rest of my career, I spent at least part of every year at Mammoth Lakes as a key part of my preparation.

I broke up the training with a fair amount of racing. I won national titles on the road and track and in cross-country that year. As late as September, just two months before New York, I placed fourth in the World Cup 5000-meter final in Madrid, Spain. On a personal level, having the range to compete over many distances and on many surfaces was important to me. Shorter races and the training needed to do well in them are compatible with marathon training, regardless of how fast you run. The different types of workouts make you a more complete runner; being efficient at 5K and 10K race pace makes marathon pace feel easier. But not *too* easy—after a 15-mile tempo run at marathon pace, I asked my teammate Deena Kastor, "How am I supposed to keep this five-minutes-per-mile pace for another eleven miles?"

CAN'T FIGHT THE FEELING

Despite my training and talking with experienced marathoners, I was surprised by how easy the early miles were. I was used to running 5Ks and 10Ks, where you're breathing hard and concentrating on keeping up your pace almost from the start. Now I was focusing on the opposite—not running too fast. The excitement of the day and my pre-race taper made the first several miles feel like I was on a training run, not in the lead pack of the world's largest marathon running faster than 5:00 per mile. It was hard not to feel a little like I was cheating as we passed halfway in 1:03:48. I knew there was a long way to go, but I felt like I could hold this pace forever.

Coach Larsen and I had heard all about miles 17–19 on First Avenue in Manhattan. It's often a key stretch of the race. You come off the Queensboro Bridge, with its rise and fall and cross-winds, to a wide road with a gentle downhill slope. First Avenue occurs at the point in many marathons where the first big moves of the race are made. The moves tend to be much more aggressive at that point in New York because it's the fastest part of the course. I was under strict orders from Coach Larsen to keep my cool.

I was running near Mark Carroll of Ireland, who I knew from racing against in college, when the moves started. That year's Boston Marathon champion, Rodgers Rop of Kenya, was up front pushing the pace. Mark held back. Me, well, I ignored my coach's advice and got up with the leaders. Then I took the lead. I ran a 4:40 mile, then a 4:30 mile, more like 10K pace than marathon pace. I felt great!

One reason I went to the lead: the huge crowds that line First Avenue. I had never experienced their combination of loudness and energy before, even in the 83,000-person stadium at the 2000 Olympics in Sydney, Australia. On First Avenue, the crowds are right there at your level, crammed close to the road, all shouting over each other for three straight miles. I could hear my name being called, I could hear "USA! USA!" I thought, "All right, this is kind of fun. This marathon thing is for me."

My move winnowed the lead pack to Rop, me, and two others. I told myself I had a shot at winning and that, at worst, I'd finish fourth. A little before mile 20, I took off my beanie, gloves, and arm warmers and threw them to the side of the road.

I tossed a cup of water on my head. It was finally time for the real racing to start.

TWENTY MILES IS HALFWAY

I ran my first marathon in the racing shoes I used for shorter road races. The lighter the better, I figured. And that was true for much of the race—but as we left the excitement of First Avenue and still had 10K to go, I started to realize otherwise. The lack of cushioning became a hindrance, not a help. I was now feeling the ground much more with every step. I felt like I was stomping into the road rather than getting a nice quick pop with each step, as I had been just a couple of miles earlier. After the race my father told me he'd thought I needed more-cushioned shoes to go 26.2 miles, but he didn't want to tell me beforehand so as to not put negative thoughts in my head.

Unfortunately, I was quite capable of having negative thoughts all by myself. By mile 22 I lost contact with the lead pack. I realized I wasn't going to win. I focused on holding on to fourth place. But I was slowing drastically. It felt like people were passing me right and left, even though "only" five did by the finish.

Mark Carroll caught up to me right after we entered Central Park, with a little more than 2 miles to go. He said, "Come on, Meb." I said, "Mark, go ahead. I'm finished. I'm done."

It was a surreal experience. I'd never struggled at the end of a race while being able to speak in complete sentences. To be not out of breath but unable to pick up the pace was just something completely foreign to me, with my background in shorter races on the track. My mind said "go" and my body said "oh no." Later I likened it to having someone come to buy your car, only for the car to not start for the first time in months. Things were working fine just a little while ago; now nothing was happening.

The mental strain was also novel to me. In a 5K or 10K I had lots of experience of talking myself through tough situations, such as "Get through this lap and then you have only two more to go." On the streets of New York I was able to do that for a mile or so. But that got me only to the 23-mile mark. I still had more than 5K, and all of the Central Park section, to go. The negative thoughts fed on each other and made my physical duress that much worse.

I wound up running the final 10K in a little under 37 minutes, or just under 6:00 per mile, close to my normal training pace. I finished in 2:12:35. That's a solid debut if your only concern is time, but I've always been about competing for place. That part of the experience stung. Rop won in 2:08:17, and Mark was sixth in 2:10:54. In other words, Rop covered the last 10K more than four minutes faster than me, and Mark had put more than a minute and a half on me in just the last 2 miles. My time was also 35 seconds short of the Olympic "A" standard in the marathon. So if I did want to consider the event for the 2004 Games, I would need to run another one and finish under 2:12.

MISTAKES WERE MADE

Not that I had any interest in the 2004 Olympic Marathon, or any other marathon, after finishing. I was cold, stiff, exhausted, and mentally drained. My parents were present, and they felt sorry for me. My father tried to defrost me by massaging my legs. My mother simply said, "You don't need to do marathons." I couldn't argue with that.

That evening I did my usual post-race analysis. My choice of shoes was one mistake. Getting rid of my gloves, hat, and arm warmers was another. It certainly didn't help that I threw water on my head in 38-degree weather. That move and the lack of clothing really came back to bite me after I hit the Wall. Over the last 10K I was running about a minute per mile slower than earlier in the race, so I wasn't producing as much heat. As I got colder I tightened up that much more.

My biggest mistake, however, was ignoring all the advice I'd received about holding back before mile 20 no matter how good I felt. It was unrealistic of me, in my first marathon, to be the aggressor on First Avenue and not think there would be negative consequences. Certainly, if you ignore reality in a 5K, you'll pay for it. If you make the common mistake of running the first half mile much faster than you can sustain for 3.1 miles, you'll pay back that time gain, and then some, in the last mile. But that final mile won't be one of the most miserable experiences of your life, and you won't be sore and exhausted, and possibly injured, in the following days.

In New York, I learned that expending your energy too early in the marathon has a far greater cost. I wrote in my log, "Be ready for a move at mile 24, not 16." Now I tell people that if you can pick it up the last mile of a marathon you've done a good job of rationing your resources. Being able to do that means you won't be dragging the several previous miles, you'll finish passing people, and you'll end on a high note that will whet your appetite for more.

I had the opposite experience that first time. Finishing New York was the hardest thing I'd ever done in running. I was prepared physically, and enjoyed that part of the process. I made a huge mental error that led to more suffering than seemed necessary. Overall, putting all that effort into a race that could go so wrong so quickly just didn't seem worth it.

The next day I felt the same. (Mentally, that is; physically,

I felt even worse.) I thought, "Why?! Why would I want to do that again? It's not fun, it's not satisfying, it's not healthy." Being a student of the sport, I knew that "never again" was a common pledge after a marathon and that it was often broken. Coach Larsen said, "I've heard that one before." But I meant it.

As the days went by I remained disenchanted with the marathon. Then I took a trip that changed my perspective on the race, and as a result changed my life.

KEY LESSON

You don't have to swing for the fences in everything you do. Cruise control can be an effective, low-stress way not only to run your fastest but to reach your full potential in many areas of life.

Two weeks after my first marathon, I traveled to Eritrea with my mom. It was the first time I'd been back to the land of my birth since we left when I was ten years old. That reconnection with my past wound up playing a huge role in my future.

I saw how hard daily life is for most people in Eritrea, especially in the rural areas like the one where I grew up. People get water from wells that might be miles away. They're constantly looking for wood to build fires for cooking and heat. They drive teams of donkeys loaded up with hay through mountains, some-times doing so by moonlight.

It's not that I'd forgotten these things from my childhood. But seeing them so soon after running my first marathon in one of the world's greatest cities was striking. People in Eritrea live like this, day in and day out, just to survive, I told myself. I thought about what I'd experienced in my marathon. That was temporary discomfort, I realized, not permanent pain. Also, I told myself, I had a choice—nobody put a gun to my head and said, "You have to run a marathon or finish it." The people I saw in Eritrea had no choice in how they spent their days. So yes, I'd been miserable for maybe forty minutes in my debut mara-thon, but I had no room to complain. My experiences in Eritrea helped me realize I could go through temporary pain again for another chance to see if I could succeed in the marathon. I real-ized I should give the distance another shot.

Why the marathon? Why didn't I see how hard life in Eritrea is and rededicate myself to being the best 10K runner I could be? For one thing, I wanted to be the Haile Gebrselassie of the United States. Like Haile, from Ethiopia, who set world records at distances from 2000 meters indoors to the marathon, I wanted to be a versatile runner. I wanted to be the best American on the track, in cross-country, and on the roads. Being a complete runner like Haile meant running the marathon. I think rededi-cating to the marathon was also influenced by the experience of running so well for the first 21 miles in NYC. There was a lot of potential; it just needed to be polished. And if you can succeed in the marathon, it's more financially lucrative and much more popular than the track.

My time in Eritrea also helped me see the marathon as more than just another race. More than any other event, the marathon is about tenacity, durability, and trying daily to get the best out of yourself. Those are qualities that people around the world can relate to, whether you're an Eritrean struggling to feed your family or an American trying to be a good parent and get ahead at work. As with life, the marathon can involve pain and agony, but it can also bring rewards of exhilaration and achievement for persevering. I wanted to return to the marathon not only to challenge myself but also, I hoped, to accomplish things that would inspire others to try their best in running and life.

SEEKING THE STANDARD

I came home from six weeks in Eritrea fired up. The Boston Marathon was three months away, and I told Coach Larsen I wanted to do it. "What got into you?" he asked in response. I told him about my realization in Eritrea. I was young, I was fit, I was eager to do what I'd told myself I should be doing. Plus, even then, the Boston Marathon was always in my heart. In 2002 I almost purchased a house in Claremont, California, a mile from San Diego's Mission Bay Park, because I thought the hills in the area would prepare me for the Boston course. I even offered $7,500 over the asking price because I was convinced this was where I could train properly for Boston. (Never mind that I hadn't even seen the Boston course at that time.)

Coach Larsen reminded me of the big picture. The 2004 Olympic Marathon Trials would be held in February 2004 in Birmingham, Alabama, with the top three finishers representing the United States at that summer's Olympics in Athens, Greece. But there was a caveat: The United States could send three men in the event only if all three had run under the Olympic "A" standard of 2:12:00. That seems straightforward, but in 2000, when the same rules were in effect, the United States had sent only one man (and, it turned out, one woman) to the Sydney Olympics. Both of the Trials races that year were hot and won in slow times. USA Track & Field, the sport's governing body, had a policy that the winners of the Trials would go to Sydney even if they didn't have the "A" standard. Going into the Trials, neither of the races' eventual winners, Rod DeHaven and Christine Clark, had the "A" standard, and they didn't achieve it in the Trials.

What this meant four years later was that it was crucial to have the "A" standard before the Trials. You didn't want to count on the Trials race being fast enough to attain it there, especially because Trials marathons are always about place, not time. So now that I was going to give the marathon another try, the main goal in my next one was to run faster than that "A" standard of 2:12:00. I'd fallen 35 seconds short in my debut. Coach Larsen told me that Boston was a tough course, and the weather was often detrimental to running fast. He convinced me to temper my newfound enthusiasm and wait until the fall to run the Chicago Marathon, a race known for its flat course and fast times.

RUNNING ON CRUISE CONTROL

Meeting my goal in Chicago meant running differently than I had in almost every race of my life. No matter what distance, I had always run to win or compete with the leaders as well as I could. That was even my approach when I ran my debut marathon in New York. Although I struggled mightily at the end of that race, I didn't regret going in with a "run to win" mind-set. I just went about trying to win the wrong way, by pushing too soon.

In Chicago, my approach would be different: I was there solely to run faster than 2:12. With the leaders aiming for a time more like 2:05, I would let them go from the start and run my own race. My second marathon wound up being my most unusual for this reason. It was the only one of twenty-six where even before the start I knew I'd make no effort to run with the leaders.

The race organizers arranged a pacer to help me meet my time goal. Godfrey Kiprotich of Kenya was an accomplished road racer at shorter distances who was finishing out his career as a pacer, or rabbit, in marathons. The plan was for Godfrey to run with me for the first 16 miles or so at slightly faster than 2:12 marathon pace. After that he would step off the course and it would be up to me to stay on pace for the last 10 miles.

The early miles went as planned. It was odd—and, I admit, a little difficult—to watch the lead group separate themselves from Godfrey and me almost immediately. I reminded myself why I was there, to get that Olympic "A" standard, and that I'd have plenty of other chances to race like I usually did.

After about 8 miles, Godfrey said his hamstring felt tight and that he was going to end his rabbiting early. He said he was supposed to be a pacer at the New York City Marathon a few weeks later and didn't want to risk getting a big injury before. So now I would be running the last 18 miles, not the last 10, by myself.

I didn't really mind doing so, to be honest. I had my watch set to show each mile split rather than the total time. If you run 5:00 per mile for a marathon, you finish in just over 2:11. Running that pace on the flat streets of Chicago, at sea level, felt very easy after having done long tempo runs at that pace at altitude in hilly Mammoth Lakes. After Godfrey stopped running with me, the biggest challenge was not going too fast. Sometimes I would run a 4:50 mile and think, "Too fast, slow down." Then I might run a 5:10 and think, "Oops, too slow, pick it up a little." Occasionally I struggled to get in the right 5:00-per-mile rhythm.

But mostly I enjoyed myself, running what felt more like a tempo run than a race. I kept holding back, holding back, mindful of my New York City experience of hitting the Wall from pushing the pace too soon. I was thinking only about the finish line and the clock, not whose moves I should cover, whether to surge to try to break up the pack, all those things that I usually think about when competing. Although I moved up from fourteenth at halfway to eventually finish seventh, even those late-race passes were different—they just sort of happened while I went about chasing my time goal, rather than me fighting to overtake someone after spotting him up ahead of me.

Like I said, I was looking only at my mile splits, not the total time. So it wasn't until the final stretch, when I saw the finish line clock, that I realized how close I was to breaking 2:10. I finished in 2:10:03, more than two and a half minutes faster than a year earlier in New York City. I was ecstatic. I'd easily met my time goal, and by a large margin while feeling comfortable the whole way. The run felt so much more like a tempo run than a race that I did a ten-minute cool-down jog. I thought, "Hey, I guess the marathon can be fun!"

LEARNING FROM HOLDING BACK

Although I never ran another marathon this way, my run in Chicago taught me a lot. I greatly improved my best time despite not going all out. (In fact, my time was the fastest by an American for the year.) This result drove home that patience is a virtue in marathoning and in life. I realized it's possible to achieve great things by staying controlled instead of always swinging for the fences. Sprinters talk about relaxing and letting the speed come out. They mean that they can only reach their potential by not straining, both mentally and physically.

That's true in so many parts of life. Doing your best means being dedicated to putting in the work, dedicated to meeting your goals. Often the most effective way to do that is to quietly but consistently go about your business at a sustainable level. Our society tends to celebrate those who take that one bold chance, who risk everything at one do-or-die moment. Sure, that can lead to amazing results. But we usually don't hear about the people who act that way and fail. In much of life, the better approach is that of a patient investor, steadily building assets over time, as opposed to going for extraordinary returns and risk crashing.

I really internalized this lesson in training. Chicago built my confidence that if I stayed relaxed and did solid work week after week after week, great things would be possible. I've trained with people who ran amazing workouts but were seldom able to run races at the same level of quality. After Chicago, I was never again someone who tried to get a gold medal for workouts. Always pushing as hard as you can is more likely to lead to injury or being overtrained than to peak performance. The repeated right efforts are what bring results and confidence. When I'm asked the secret to my success, I often say there is no secret, but the key is consistency. If I regularly got in my key workouts of long runs, tempo runs, and intervals at a good-but-not-amazing level, I felt like I could compete with anybody in the world. And that was exactly what I intended to do at the following year's Olympics in Athens.

But I'm getting ahead of myself. First I had to make the Olympic team at the Trials race in February. Having achieved the "A" standard in Chicago, I could return to my usual approach, competing against others, at the Trials. After a short break from running after Chicago, I began my buildup for the Trials in Birmingham. I was feeling fit and confident.

That feeling didn't last.

2004 OLYMPIC MARATHON TRIALS
(Birmingham, Alabama)

FEBRUARY 7, 2004

PLACE **2nd**   TIME **2:11:47**

KEY LESSON

Underpromise and overdeliver.

B efore big races you'll often hear elite runners publicly state ambitious goals. They'll say they're going to win, or run a really fast time, or beat a certain person. You might do this in your own running or in other parts of your life, telling anyone who will listen that you're going to run a personal best in your next half marathon, or get your dream job, or lose 20 pounds. The idea is that sharing "reach" goals with many people makes the goal more real to you and makes you more accountable to others. You'll be a lot more likely to stick with your diet, the thinking goes, if you know a lot of people will be seeing whether you look slimmer.

That's never been my approach. Of course I set really big goals—I started almost every race of my life thinking that I had a shot to win. But I never talked like that in pre-race interviews. Before I won the 2014 Boston Marathon, I told a handful of close associates soon before the race that I would be running for the victory. But I didn't even tell my brother Hawi, who is also my manager!

Another high-profile instance of applying this idea to running is when I set the American record for 10,000 meters in May 2001. The period before the race was my first extended training stint at altitude. There, because there's less oxygen in the air, all your paces are slower for the same effort. It's easy to feel like you're simultaneously tired from the training and out of shape. Breaking the U.S. 10K record was one of my eventual goals, but I didn't feel like I was ready to do so at that year's Cardinal Invitational. I kept a very low profile before the race. On the morning of the race, my good friend Mike Long, who helped found the Rock 'n' Roll race series, told me that Bob Kennedy was going for the American record. Only then did I say, "Well, I guess he'll have to beat me to do it." And that was in a private conversation with someone close to me. So when I finished fourth behind three Kenyans in 27:13.98 to break a record that had stood for almost fifteen years, the impact was that much greater because it shocked so many people.

Part of my habit of speaking modestly about my goals comes from my upbringing. The culture of Eritrea is built on accountability and delivering results. Hawi and I and our siblings were raised that it's not right to go around saying, "I'm going to do this, I'm going to do that." In Eritrea, what matters is what you do, not what you say you're going to do. Growing up poor reinforced that actions speak louder than words—when you have few resources to draw on, you usually look foolish promising the sun and the moon. What's better, our parents told us (and showed by example), is to be humble, modest, and hardworking, and then surprise people with how well you've done something. Underpromise and overdeliver. Fortunately,

Coach Larsen, with his humble roots in Minnesota, also had this approach.

I never implemented that lesson more than in my third marathon, the 2004 Olympic Trials.

A PERSONAL RECORD, THEN PANIC

Like I said, my big personal best in Chicago didn't take much out of me. I was nonetheless cautious afterward and took some downtime. A month after the race, I was still doing only 70 miles a week, well below the 120 weekly miles I'd run preparing for Chicago. The fitness I'd built for Chicago was still there—I just needed to bring it back before the Trials in early February. At that race in Birmingham, Alabama, if I finished in the top three, I would be on the Olympic team in the marathon.

Things initially went well when I started to ramp up. In early December, with two months to go to the Trials, I felt good during a 99-mile week. (Yes, I thought about doing another mile at the end of the week to get to 100.) But then both knees started bothering me. The right-knee problems lingered longer and gave me more trouble. I had to make frequent stops on runs because the right knee was so painful. By the middle of December I had knee tendinitis. It wasn't bad enough to prevent running, but it wasn't mild enough to allow normal training. I would run 6 or 8 miles a day, but just at an easy-to-moderate pace. I couldn't do the tempo runs or other quality workouts I needed to be ready to race the best U.S. marathoners. The knee felt worse, not better, after runs, which is never a good sign.

Around this time I also caught the flu. I don't get sick often, but when I do, I get really sick. A few days before Christmas I took some powerful medicine. During my professional career,

I was subject to frequent drug testing, both at races and out of competition. I fully support this testing as a way to catch and deter runners who want to cheat by taking performance-enhancing drugs. But because of the frequent testing, I almost never took medications, because of the fear they might contain substances that are prohibited. On the rare occasion I did take medicine, that meant I was really sick and that the medication would affect me more than people who are used to taking it.

So I didn't have a very merry Christmas. With the Trials a month and a half away, I told Coach Larsen I thought I should scratch my entry. I wasn't running much, and what running I was doing wasn't of the quality I needed to finish in the top three at the Trials. I was also worried that running the Trials marathon without being ready could make my knee injury worse or give me some other injury that I would then have to deal with. I told Bob I thought a better plan was to skip the Trials and focus on making the 10,000-meter Olympic team on the track, like I'd done in 2000.

Coach Larsen encouraged me to be patient. "Maybe things will turn around," he told me. If not, I could withdraw from the Trials much closer to race day, he said. Thank God for Bob's advice, because it paid off in a big way.

By the second week of January I was able to start adding a little quality to my running. A 10K tempo run in 32:16 was nothing compared to what I'd been doing before Chicago, but it was something. Before the Trials I had time to increase to a 10-mile tempo run at a little faster than marathon race pace. My longest run was 20 miles, compared to 24 or 25 miles as I'd done before my first two marathons. I ran twice a day only a few times during my entire buildup, compared to usually doing so six days a week. To supplement the running I was able to do, I biked a lot.

RACING INTO THE UNKNOWN

If ever there was a time to underpromise and overdeliver, it was in Birmingham. Before my first marathon, I'd had a lot of doubts about whether my body could go the 26.2-mile distance. At the Trials, with two marathons behind me, I knew I could finish. The uncertainty was how my body would hold up at race pace. My tempo runs were much shorter than before my other marathons, and my longest run was what I used to do every week when training for the 10K. I was severely undertrained. Never mind what I told others—even to myself I thought, "Third place is as good as first; just make the team." All I cared about was getting one of those first three spots; I didn't care which one.

My race plan was to play it by ear, given all the uncertainty. If six people made a break from the lead pack 10 miles into the race, should I go with them? Normally that wouldn't even be a question—of course I would cover that move, because some of the six will be able to maintain the pace until the end, so if I didn't go with them my chance of finishing in the top three was small. But this time, I wasn't sure how my body would hold up to covering a strong move at that point in the race with so many miles left to run.

Another element of uncertainty: Most of the field didn't have the Olympic "A" standard of 2:12:00 or faster that I'd attained in Chicago. If they wanted to run in the Olympics, they would almost certainly have to run faster than 2:12 in the Trials race. That worried me, because I wasn't sure I was in shape to break 2:12, especially in an unevenly paced race on a course with many turns like Birmingham's.

Brian Sell was one of those guys who needed the "A" standard. He made a huge move to break away from the lead pack at about 8 miles into the race. Brian was an up-and-coming runner who hadn't yet developed into a world-class marathoner. None of the top contenders, like Alan Culpepper, who had the fastest qualifying time, or Dan Browne, covered Brian's move. Only Teddy Mitchell, another one who needed the "A" standard, went with him. As much as not going with Brian was against my "run to win" nature, I was relieved that the field let him go. It was unlikely that both Brian and Teddy would be able to hold off everyone else until the finish.

After a few miles, Teddy was unable to keep with Brian and eventually dropped out of the race. That left Brian alone in front with a huge lead. By the 15th mile, the chase group was down to Alan, Dan, and me. Four guys fighting for three spots wasn't a good scenario for me and my lack of training. Coach Larsen was on the side of the road somewhere in the 18th mile. "Go now, go now!" he yelled. Who says you can't get good advice from the sidelines? I love hearing words of encouragement and technical advice from my family, friends, and coaches. Bob's urging was great advice—if the three of us worked together to chase down Brian, we could catch him far enough before the finish that we should be able to drop him.

I picked up the pace. Alan and Dan knew exactly what I was doing and went with me. We worked hard for the next 5K to reel in Brian. In a scenario like this, the best approach is to go hard but not all out. You want to catch the guy you're chasing down and pass him with enough momentum that he's unable to go with you. But you still have a race to finish. Especially in the Trials, where third place is as good as first, you don't want to push so hard that if someone comes from behind in the last mile you can't defend that final Olympic team spot. I knew what I was doing was the right strategy, but I was still unsure if I had the fitness to properly execute it.

RACING INSTINCTS KICK IN

We caught Brian in the 22nd mile. He was unable to respond, and we passed him like he was standing still, which was a huge relief to me. Brian had given his all and eventually faded to finish twelfth (once Eddy Hellebuyck was removed from the results after receiving a doping violation). After the race I told Brian to stick with it, that he'd be an Olympian the next time around. Brian's courage and work ethic were rewarded four years later when he placed third at the 2008 Olympic Marathon Trials and ran in the Beijing Games. That was a great accomplishment for someone who hadn't been a star runner in high school or college. It was also a testament to the Hansons-Brooks program, the training group that recruited and developed Brian.

My natural racing instincts took over once we dispatched Brian. I kept pushing for the next two miles in the hope of breaking Alan and Dan. Doing so half worked—Dan fell off in the 25th mile. I told myself I was going to be on the team. Alan and I slowed a little to catch our breath after that long surge the last several miles.

If I'd been fitter, I would have kept the pressure on and gone for the kill with so little of the race left. My lack of training meant I needed to briefly recover before going for the win. After 25 miles I tried to get away from Alan, who had always had a great kick over the last lap on the track. But I didn't have the turnover I needed to gap Alan.

We entered the final 600 meters together. He made a move that I covered. I made a move that he covered. Then he flat-out sprinted for a short distance. It was a classic track racing move—sprint for 50 meters at the start of the last lap to get a gap, and then all you have to do is run the same pace as your pursuers the rest of the race. Alan won in 2:11:42. I finished second, 5 seconds back in 2:11:47. Dan rounded out the team in 2:12:02. Alan later said if I'd made one more move in the final stretch he would have let me go. I told him, "I wish I'd known that at the time!"

DO IT, THEN SAY IT

I was ecstatic to make my second Olympic team. Earning that berth six months before the Games in Athens gave me freedom and options. Freedom, in that I could spend the time before Athens doing what was best for my performance in the Olympics. Options, in that now Coach Larsen and I could explore whether I should concentrate on the marathon, focus instead on running the 10K in Athens, or run both events in the Olympics.

Running both events was tempting. I got excited thinking about taking on the world's best twice within a little more than a week. But while Coach Larsen and I spent a fair amount of time discussing running that double, I didn't talk about it publicly. There's another good reason to underpromise and overdeliver: Why put more pressure on yourself? We runners are highly motivated. We're often our own harshest critics. We put enough pressure on ourselves; why add to it by telling the world what you hope to do? There were times during my career when I felt I was capable of running 2:05 in the marathon. But you won't find any interviews in which I say that. Before my marathon debut, I never said I was going for the U.S. debut record. Did I know what that time was? Absolutely. Did I say that's what I was going to do? No. Underpromise and overdeliver is especially good advice before your first time trying something, because you don't know what's waiting for you.

So while I dreamed about medaling in two events, I kept quiet. I knew I'd rather say I'd accomplished something at the Olympics than talk about what I was going to accomplish there.

Saying what you're going to do in the future ignores the fact that a completely different future is just one injury away. I certainly became familiar with that reality before the Olympic Marathon Trials in Birmingham. Now that I had overdelivered in Birmingham, it was time to turn my attention to Athens.

2004 OLYMPIC MARATHON
(Athens, Greece)

AUGUST 29, 2004

PLACE   **2nd**   TIME   **2:11:29**

KEY LESSON

Experience isn't everything. Have belief in your abilities and confidence in your preparation.

E xperience is valuable in most parts of life. Later on I'll tell the stories of marathons where my experience at the distance helped me outperform people who "should" have beaten me in those races. As my career progressed, experiences I had in training and racing helped me make better decisions on how to work toward my goals. In general, I'd prefer that the people fixing my car, doing my taxes, and educating my daughters aren't just starting out.

But experience can be overrated. Being relatively new to something can mean putting fewer limits on yourself. You might also be more motivated to do your best the third time you take on a challenge than the thirtieth. There's an interesting history of top runners excelling early in their marathon careers.

Paula Radcliffe of Great Britain won the London Marathon and almost broke the world record in her debut. She then set world records in her next two marathons. Alberto Salazar won the first four marathons of his career—three times in New York City, once at Boston. Even at the Olympics, Emil Zatopek of Czechoslovakia won the marathon at the 1952 Games in his first go at the distance, and John Treacy of Ireland took silver in the 1984 Olympics in his marathon debut.

As a student of the sport, I was aware of this history as I went about preparing for the 2004 Olympics. My experience in Athens is an example of how working hard and believing in yourself can get you far even if you're not a veteran at something. You'll never know if your time has come if you don't try!

DECIDING ON MY DISTANCE

I came out of the Olympic Marathon Trials in great shape. It sounds odd, but my recovery was quick because I'd entered the race so undertrained. My legs weren't beat up from lots of high mileage, and I was fresh mentally. In the month following the marathon trials I won the national 8K and 15K titles on the roads. From there I kept building—including second place to a world half marathon champion at the Bolder Boulder 10K in May—toward July's Olympic 10,000-Meter Trials.

At the track trials I successfully defended my 10K title from four years earlier. I was in the shape of my life. I was the American record holder in the 10K and had years of experience in that event. In contrast, I'd run only three marathons. In the first I'd hit the Wall. The second, I ran more like a workout than a race. I entered the third undertrained and uncertain. Which event should I run in the Olympics?

On paper, the 10K looked like the better choice. That was

what Billy Mills, the last American to win the event in the Olympics, urged me to do. For a week after the track trials I thought about doubling—running the 10K, followed by the marathon nine days later. At that point either you're fit or you're not. The 10K could serve as my last hard effort during a time when I'd already be resting up for the marathon.

Ultimately I decided to run only the marathon. I didn't want an outcome like finishing fourth in the 10K and fourth in the marathon, and then think, "If I'd done only one race . . ." and regret it for the rest of my life. I'd rather concentrate on one thing and do it well. I felt I had an opportunity to bring home a medal for the United States and shouldn't jeopardize my chances. The three most prestigious events at the Olympics are the 100 meters, the 1500 meters (aka "the metric mile") and the marathon. There was also the pull of the marathon course— along the route that gave the race its name, from Marathon to Athens, finishing in Panathinaiko Stadium, which hosted the first modern Olympics in 1896.

PREPARATION BREEDS CONFIDENCE

My training for Athens was almost seamless. Every week I felt stronger and faster. And every week I got more and more ex- cited about my chances to medal. What was especially motivat- ing was that I was running amazing times in training despite my policy of not racing workouts. I still remember one key ses- sion like it was yesterday. I averaged 4:57 per mile for a 15-mile tempo run at 7,000 feet of altitude. That's the first 15 miles of a 2:10 marathon, in the middle of hard training, in oxygen-scarce air. I told myself that nobody I'd face in Athens was doing any better than that. This wasn't ego or self-delusion, just a simple reading of the facts. Before any big task you're relatively new to, if you're doing your homework, you should feel ready for what lies ahead.

Part of my homework for Athens was to be ready to race in the heat. Some people predicted that the temperature during the marathon would reach 100. On my easy training days I ran at noon in extra layers of clothing to simulate running in the heat. I wore a normal amount of clothing for my hard workouts and long runs, and stuck with doing those key sessions in the morning. It was important to be acclimated to the heat, but not at the expense of the quality of my training.

On the advice of Dr. Mike Karch, I also got ready for the heat by sitting in a sauna. He was a veteran of the Badwater Marathon, a 135-mile race that starts in Death Valley, one of the hottest places in the world. I started with 10 minutes in the sauna, shirtless. From there I was to build to 20 minutes with a T-shirt on, then 25, then 30. When I got to half an hour, he said, I should sit in the sauna in layers of clothing—a long-sleeve shirt over the T-shirt, then a sweater on top of that, then a track suit, all while increasing my sauna time to an hour.

There's an important lesson here: We all get advice, on pretty much everything we do in life. You always need to weigh it to see if it works for your situation. Yes, it was a good idea to get better at sweating and to become more accustomed to being uncomfortably warm. But Dr. Karch's advice was based on what worked for him to jog/walk 135 miles in some of the most extreme heat in the world. I was preparing to race the best runners in the world in above-average temperatures for a marathon. I didn't need to overdo it in the sauna just for the sake of overdoing it. I needed to adapt the general advice to my needs. I wound up topping out at 30 minutes (which, believe me, is still plenty with a shirt on).

I took to heart another piece of advice that has general implications. When I was in college, Olympians Steve Scott and

Ruth Wysocki had told me that if I made it to the Olympics, I should run the event like any other race. It's the Olympics, but don't freak out and feel like you need to reinvent the wheel, they told me; instead, keep doing what got you there.

I'd already noticed that some people overdo it before the Olympics. They think, "I need to up my game, I have to do this, I have to do that, I have to work much harder than I ever have." For a lot of people, this mentality results in becoming over-trained or injured by the time they get to the Olympics. The same thing happens with everyday runners preparing for the Boston or New York City Marathon or other once-in-a-lifetime challenges. They forget it's the same body doing the same ac-tivity. Yes, the platform is higher, but it's not like you should suddenly double your workouts. I'm not saying don't dream or be willing to work hard. But keep things simple, effective, and within your means. Part of working hard is having the discipline to know when enough is enough. Grow your capabilities over time, not suddenly two months before a big race.

The only hiccup in my preparation occurred ten days before the marathon. While on a training run, I had to leap to avoid a charging dog. The incident wound up leading to some tendinitis in my right knee. I tried to stay calm and told myself the hard work was behind me, and that with the reduced running I'd be doing anyway, it probably wouldn't be an issue by race day. Eas-ier said than done, of course. On the afternoon of the race I was still uncertain. I even called my brother Hawi and told him if I didn't finish, don't worry, I'm just playing it safe with the knee.

NO NEWBIE NERVOUSNESS

When I was a freshman at UCLA, Coach Larsen would tell me, "Just go out there and have fun. The pressure's not on you.

Chase those people who are expected to win." That's how I felt on race day in Athens. I was flying under the radar. It was the guys with the long marathon résumés who were feeling the pressure of expectations. It's common when you're relatively in-experienced at something to feel nervous or uptight about how you're going to do. I think a better approach is to stay relaxed. Let the veterans feel the weight of expectations. If you've pre-pared properly, be confident that your best will be good enough. I was confident enough that I arranged to have the medal cer-emony jacket we all received as part of our U.S. uniform waiting for me at the finish line.

I was also newly inspired to run well because of two earlier races in the Games. My Mammoth Lakes teammate Deena Kas-tor won the bronze medal in the marathon the previous week. Her result gave me great confidence that the work we had done over the summer was the right preparation for Athens. In the men's 10K, Zersenay Tadese of Eritrea won the bronze medal. He was the first Eritrean to win an Olympic medal. I felt proud to see someone from my native land perform so well on the world stage.

The main person I planned to key off was Paul Tergat of Kenya. The previous fall, he had run 2:04:55 at the Berlin Mara-thon to become the first person to break 2:05 for the distance. His race pace compared to my personal best meant that I would have literally been more than a mile behind him when he fin-ished. But while I greatly respected Paul, I didn't fear him—or anyone else on the start line in Athens.

For one thing, I knew my personal best of 2:10:03 didn't reflect my full ability. I'd run Chicago under control, far from all out, to get the sub-2:12 Olympic "A" standard. I felt I was capable of running two or three minutes faster. So although my personal record (PR) was only the 38th best out of the 101 start-ers in Athens, I didn't consider that an accurate gauge of where

I stood in the field. I also reminded myself that even those with faster PRs were highly unlikely to run close to those times in a hot, hilly race where place, not time, is what matters. I figured I really just needed to beat one-third of the field—one-third would be overtrained from trying to produce magic for the Olympics, and the other third would be struggling with injuries or psychological problems (again because of trying to go above and beyond for the Olympics).

The temperature was in the mid-80s for the start. I did just a one-mile warm-up jog, a mile or two shorter than usual. I figured the race would start slowly and I could use the early miles to get into my rhythm. With a six p.m. start time, the temperature would fall during the race and radiant heat from sunlight wouldn't be an issue.

When the gun went off, I was immediately in the zone. The knee tendinitis from the dog attack was never an issue. I started at the back of the pack—the only time I did so in my marathon career—and slowly worked my way through the field. I didn't join the lead group until around the 20K mark.

RISING TO THE OCCASION

I'll admit I had a few pinch-myself moments as I passed halfway among the leaders. To be shoulder to shoulder with Paul Tergat was an honor. I'd looked up to him as a role model, and early in my career I had picked his brain about training, racing, and any other topic he wanted to tell me about. At one point I looked around and thought how cool it was that I was there running with Paul, two other Kenyans, three Ethiopians, and other top marathoners in the world. I was among the best, trying to be the best I could be.

It was too early in the race to know whether I'd be in medal contention later. It was time to settle in and settle down, and not be awed by Paul, who had once lapped me in a 10K. As planned, I keyed off him, running next to or tucked in behind him, saving my energy for the big move I thought he would make later.

It was a race of attrition, with the heat and hills taking their toll and steadily shrinking the field. (No doubt those Olympic-year injuries, overtraining, and psychological strain also played a role.) There were six of us in what I thought was the lead pack as we approached 20 miles. I told myself all I had to do was beat three of them and I'd be a medalist. All I was thinking was, "Get a medal, get a medal." I didn't care which one.

Eventually I realized we were the chase group. Vanderlei de Lima of Brazil had gapped the field at an earlier drink station and was running solo in the front. By this time we were down to five—Paul Tergat; Stefano Baldini of Italy, bronze medalist at the last two world championships; Jaouad Gharib of Morocco, who had won the world championship the year before; and Jon Brown of Great Britain, who finished fourth in the 2000 Olympic Marathon. I was, by far, the least experienced in the group at this level of marathoning.

But when you're ready and believe in yourself, the present is more telling than the past. With less than 10K to go, I realized Paul was struggling. I always watch my competitors for signs of physical distress. Paul's usual beautiful flowing stride was starting to break down; he wasn't getting that same pop off the ground as a few miles earlier. I pushed really hard to capitalize on this opportunity. Paul and Gharib fell off. Brown remained in the hunt. I thought, "One more person to beat and I'm an Olympic medalist."

With about four miles to go, Stefano and I had gotten away from Brown. De Lima was still ahead of us. Never mind that it was the Olympics and it was only my fourth marathon. This was racing 101—work together to reel in de Lima, then fight it out for the win. I pulled up alongside Stefano and said, *"Andiamo, uno e due,"* meaning, "Let's go, one and two." He looked at me like, "Who is this guy, and how does he know Italian?" I realized later I should have sprinted away right then while he was wondering what the heck was going on.

Soon after we started charging came an unforgettable moment. Cornelius Horan, a defrocked Irish priest known for disrupting events to spread his end-times message, ran from the sidelines and pushed de Lima into the crowd. Vanderlei wasn't harmed, only stunned, and as people wrestled Horan to the ground, Vanderlei resumed running.

There's been a lot of talk about whether that unfortunate incident cost Vanderlei the gold medal. I may be biased, but I don't think it did. Before the incident Stefano and I were closing fast. Both of us wound up running our last 10K at around 2:05 marathon pace. I think the incident made the inevitable happen a little sooner.

Stefano and I were still chasing down de Lima when Stefano made a big move with about 5K to go, on a little incline on an underpass. These many years later it's easy for me to say I should have gone with him. But at the time I had a flashback to my marathon debut in New York City. I thought, "5K is a long way to go." I was confident that I'd catch de Lima by maintaining my current effort. But I worried that maybe Tergat had just been having a brief bad patch when we dropped him, and he or somebody else was closing even faster than we were. If I went all out to stick with Stefano, I might pay the price in a mile or two and give someone a chance to overtake me. I reminded myself I'd come to Athens hoping to medal, and decided the surest way of making that dream come true was to let Stefano go.

Stefano passed de Lima at the 2-hour mark. Vanderlei looked back and saw that I was also about to overtake him. This reinforced to me that he wouldn't be challenging me for the silver.

With about a mile to go I was confident nobody would be sprinting past me in the remaining handful of minutes. I threw to the ground the cap I'd worn the whole race and pushed as hard as I could to catch Stefano.

I got closer, but Stefano was having a phenomenal day and never let up. He won in 2:10:55. I entered the stadium for the last few hundred meters with so many thoughts and emotions welling up. I took the silver in 2:11:29, and de Lima held on for the bronze in 2:12:11. He was a model of sportsmanship and graciousness after the race.

I crossed myself just before the finish line, thanking God for the opportunity to make full use of my abilities and preparation. That sentiment stayed me with me as the laurel wreath was placed on my head and the silver medal hung around my neck. I felt immense satisfaction at meeting my goal of bringing home a medal for the United States. I knew that my life was about to change in many ways.

2004 NEW YORK CITY MARATHON

NOVEMBER 7, 2004

PLACE **2nd**   TIME **2:09:53**

KEY LESSON

Celebrate your accomplishments but don't rest on your laurels. Use the momentum from one success to work toward others.

The immediate aftermath of the Olympic Marathon was tiring in its own right. The race ended a little after eight p.m., followed soon after by the medal ceremony. Post-race drug testing wasn't finished until midnight. (It can take a while to produce a urine sample when you've just raced a marathon in the heat.) With the marathon coming at the end of the Games, the U.S. team's flight was set to leave early the next day. We got on the bus at 2:30 a.m.—a little more than six hours after my race was over—for a flight to Frankfurt, Germany.

I was honored when U.S. Olympians from all sports gave me a standing ovation on the bus and plane. Elva Dryer and Kate O'Neill, two members of the 10K squad, talked the flight attendants into giving me a first-class seat for our plane ride. Not that everyone was in my corner—the laurel wreath from the medal ceremony had earlier been stolen when I set it aside to use the bathroom at the post-race press conference. Good thing I had my silver medal around my neck!

The wreath thief also didn't get the bouquet of flowers I'd received at the medal ceremony. I was carrying it because I planned to give it to Yordanos Asgedom, a fellow native of Eritrea, on our first date. Yordanos and I had met in San Jose, California, during the first week of July, and had talked on the phone every day since. But she lived in Tampa, Florida. I had said I would visit her right after the Olympics. After I medaled, she insisted I first go see my family in San Diego. I told her, "I'm a man of my word," and stuck with the Tampa plan. (We went to an Olive Garden, where the manager asked, "Didn't I just see you on TV?" Dinner was on the house—it's good to be an Olympic medalist.) Yordanos and I got married the following fall.

ON TO THE NEXT CHALLENGE

Maybe it was symbolic that my laurel wreath got stolen. I've never been one to coast after meeting a big goal. I'm always looking ahead to the next challenge rather than resting on my laurels.

Throughout the many years we worked together, Coach Larsen always told me to make the race plans I felt I needed to, and then he'd help me get ready to meet my goals. When I went to Athens I already knew I'd be running the New York City Marathon that fall. New York would be run only seventy days—ten weeks—after my race in Athens. The Olympics was just my fourth marathon, so I hadn't yet done a similar quick turnaround from one marathon to the next. But I believed that if I prepared properly for Athens and recovered smartly, I'd be ready to do well in New York.

After Athens, I was excited, and not just because of that first date with Yordanos. The Olympic race had started slow and finished fast. My body wasn't beat up like it would have been in a marathon where you go out hard and then slow down and suffer over the last several miles. I was able to climb the steep stairs at the Panathinaiko Stadium, where the Olympic race finished.

Some people have a letdown after accomplishing something they've been working toward for a long time. In running, you'll hear about the post-marathon blues. One way to avoid that down feeling is to have another challenge waiting for you. For me, the silver medal in Athens was a spark of energy, not a fire extinguished. When you feel that drive, you can build from one great achievement to another.

That doesn't mean I started training hard the day after Yordanos and I dined at the Olive Garden. The first part of the bridge from Athens to New York City was recovering from the Olympics. I knew I was in great shape; I didn't need to push things. When I resumed training I wouldn't be starting from scratch; I just needed to bring back the fitness that had helped me win an Olympic medal. I was also feeling relaxed because there was little external pressure on me to do well in New York. People thought I was going there as more of a victory lap than to seriously compete. I needed to control only the pressure I put on myself to excel.

One key in these situations, whether in running or other parts of life: After one big accomplishment, be as dedicated to recovering from it as you were to meeting it. Say you've completed a months-long project at work. If possible, plan to step away from that mode of working right after. A few days of doing fun things you weren't able to while busy should rejuvenate you more than a few weeks of sort of working, sort of relaxing. You can emerge refreshed from this concentrated recovery but still keep your momentum going from one big goal to the next.

I didn't resume running until the second week after Athens. And when I first got back into it, I was running only every other day. I waited until late September to get back in full training for the early-November race in New York. That was long enough to fully recover from Athens but short enough to maintain most of the fitness I'd worked so hard to build.

Then it was back to the same laser focus I'd had before the Olympics. When you're on a roll, you want to do everything in your power to keep that momentum going so that you can achieve your next goal. For example, I decided not to attend a reception at the White House for U.S. Olympians in mid-October. I didn't want the time away from altitude training and the distraction that would come from flying across the country for this short event. I also skipped my ten-year high school reunion. I wanted to win New York City, and I didn't want to look back after the race and think, "Oh, if I hadn't made that White House visit or left altitude for the reunion, maybe I would have won." (Don't worry about me, though—I went to the White House after the 2000, 2012, and 2016 Olympics, and Yordanos and I were guests at a state dinner at the White House in 2014.)

BACK TO THE FIVE BOROUGHS

The New York Road Runners (NYRR) assembled their usual top-notch field for my second go at New York. There were still fourteen of us in the lead pack at halfway, including that year's Boston Marathon champion, Timothy Cherigat of Kenya; one of Cherigat's training partners, John Yuda of Tanzania; two-time NYC winner John Kagwe; and my friend and fellow U.S.

Olympian Abdi Abdirahman, who was making his marathon debut.

The race remained uneventful until the 16th mile, on First Avenue in Manhattan. That few-mile stretch is usually where the fastest splits of the New York City Marathon are run. Sure enough, that's where Hendrick Ramaala of South Africa made a move to break up the lead pack. Hendrick was known primarily for excelling in shorter road races—he had twice medaled at the world half marathon championship—but he was no slouch in the marathon. He entered the race with a faster personal best than me and had finished in the top ten in New York City, London, and the world championships. In Athens, he had pushed the pace at around the halfway mark of the marathon but then dropped out. His move on First Avenue let me know he was eager to make amends for his Olympic disappointment.

With 8 miles to go, it was down to Hendrick, Cherigat, and me. To be honest, I was more worried about the reigning Boston champion than about Hendrick, who usually placed well in but seldom won big races. It just goes to show that you should always do your homework: I later learned Hendrick had run very fast (46:04) to win a 10-mile race in Holland in mid-September. At around the 24-mile mark Hendrick didn't go for a drink at the aid station. Cherigat and I did. Hendrick made a big push. All of a sudden I realized Cherigat wasn't responding to the move and that I needed to go after Hendrick alone.

Hendrick had used the same tactic that Alan Culpepper did at the Olympic Trials earlier that year, but for longer. He made that one huge surge to gain the lead, then eased back on the pace once he felt his lead was big enough. When someone hammers like that and makes the separation, they're usually not running any faster than you for the last stretch. But the damage is done. I chased Hendrick but couldn't close the gap. He won in 2:09:28. I finished second in 2:09:53, a 10-second personal best. Hendrick was so exhausted by the end that he ran through the wrong finish chute.

MAINTAINING MOTIVATION

Although I'm a very goal-oriented person and like to move from one challenge to the next instead of rest on my laurels, I still need to stoke that fire within. People might think that for world-class athletes, motivation comes naturally. What's really the case is that a lot of people have talent, but many struggle to find the motivation to develop that talent through consistent hard work. I like to think I'm better at that than most of my competitors, but I'm not a robot.

I've always collected and read motivational quotes. It's always good to learn from others, to get inspiration from others, to find ways to get yourself to put in your best efforts. I think the same way about finding motivation as I do about good ideas—I don't care where it comes from as long as it might help me reach my goals. I read all sorts of motivational materials, from proverbs and Bible verses to daily inspiration quotes and insights from other athletes and high achievers. I would especially draw on these materials when deep in training toward a big goal, such as six to eight weeks before a marathon. At that time I'd often be holed up at altitude in Mammoth Lakes, working hard day after day after day. The marathon was still far enough away that I sometimes needed reminders about why I was doing what I was doing. Reading about others who had persevered to achieve something great was very helpful at those times.

You can also get motivation to keep working hard from your immediate past. When I go to bed at night I briefly review my day. Doing so takes only thirty seconds to two minutes. What did I do today? How did I do overall? What can I improve on? If

I had a bad day, what caused it, and how can I do it better next time? I think about not only my running but things as a person. How was I toward other people? Was I kind to people in need? Did I make sure to think about others while still doing what I needed to do to meet my goals?

New York City was my third marathon of 2004. That year was the only time I ran three in a year. I had continued to progress from one goal to the next: Make the Olympic team in 2000? Check. Set the American record for 10,000 meters? Check. Win an Olympic medal? Check. Because I didn't get complacent, I was able to use meeting each of those goals as a stepping-stone to the next level. I had my Olympic medal, the dream of a lifetime. But I wanted more. I had finished second in my three marathons in 2004. Now I wanted to win one against the best in the world. To win a New York City or Boston Marathon was more important to me than getting another Olympic medal. That became the next big focus of my career.

2005 NEW YORK CITY MARATHON
NOVEMBER 6, 2005

PLACE **3rd**   TIME **2:09:56**

KEY LESSON

Small personal victories can show you that even greater things are possible in the future.

I originally planned to run the London Marathon in April 2005 but had to withdraw after another run-in with a dog aggravated my left Achilles tendon. The incident may have been a blessing in disguise. After three marathons in 2004, it was time to step away from the distance for a while. I still had goals on the track and at shorter races. The biggest of those was to lower my American 10,000-meter record of 27:13 to sub-27:00. Coach Larsen and I always felt that 10K training and racing helped rather than hurt my marathoning.

Well, unless you get injured. In 2005, an incident at the shorter distance wound up limiting me in my only go that year at the longer distance. However, even though I didn't get the results I wanted at the 10K or the marathon, the way things played out gave me great confidence for the future. I learned that giving your best even when you're not at your best can provide insight into what's possible when you're on top of your game.

A SEVERE SETBACK

I qualified for the 10K at that summer's world championships by finishing second in a sprint finish, a mere 0.19 second behind Abdi Abdirahman, at the U.S. championships in June. I was in phenomenal shape heading into the world meet in Helsinki, Finland. In training I was doing 400-meter repeats in 56 or 57 seconds (faster than 4:00 mile pace) with no problem. I ran 13:21 for a 5K in Norway soon before Worlds as a tune-up race and to get used to the time change from California to Europe. I felt ready to break 27:00 in Helsinki if that was how the race played out. As a backup opportunity, I planned to run the 10K at the Brussels Grand Prix meet three weeks after Worlds.

In Helsinki, I ran up front among the leaders early on. The pace was solid. Because of rain, we probably weren't going to break 27:00, but I was confident about my ability to match others over a fast final mile.

Late in the fourth kilometer I started to feel pain in my right quadriceps muscle. I had felt a little tightness there during my warm-up but didn't think much about it at the time, because I'd had no injuries leading up to the meet. The pain soon became excruciating. Despite running just as hard as before, I began slipping back through the pack. By the halfway mark I was all alone in last place. I started to worry that my quad muscle was going to completely tear or rupture. I stepped off the track in the 4th mile.

This was the first race of my life in which my name appeared in the results with a DNF, for *did not finish*, next to it. Dropping out of the world championships was wrenching. I knew logically it was the right decision—to keep running on a severe injury that hits you out of the blue is asking for trouble. Still, when your upbringing and instincts are all about persevering, quitting is tough emotionally.

The next day, imaging showed that I had a rupture in my right quad that was 2 centimeters wide and 11 centimeters long. I canceled all of my plans and immediately flew to Tampa, where Yordanos was living, for more medical advice and treatment. There I was told the injury would take eight to twelve weeks to heal.

One problem: My race at Worlds was on August 8. I was already signed up to run the New York City Marathon on November 6—a little more than twelve weeks away.

A MATTER OF PERSPECTIVE

I took stock of my situation. Reflecting on New York City the previous year, when I'd finished second just ten weeks after the Olympics, gave me confidence. There was an instance where I'd been able to run well with a limited buildup, thanks to already being in great shape. The same was true of when I got injured before the Olympic Trials. Rather than wallow in self-pity, I took a "the glass is half full" view: I'm starting with a good base. Now how much can I build on it while letting my leg heal? Walking is better than not being able to walk. Riding a bike and running with no impact in the pool is better than not being able to cross-train. Eventually, jogging will be better than walking, and then running will be better than jogging.

On September 7, a month after Worlds, I ran for half an hour. New York City was two months away. In any situation where you feel the clock is ticking—running or otherwise—you can't think, "I have only this amount of time to go, I absolutely have to do this, I have to do that." You have to work based on where things stand today, and how you can improve from there. In September 2005, it would have been disastrous to try to copy my training from two months before the Olympics. I needed to do what I could and be motivated by any progress. Any improvement was a sign that things were moving in the right direction.

This experience taught me another important lesson that I followed the rest of my career. People talk about going the extra mile, about how doing so is a sign of how dedicated you are. I thought, "No, go one less mile. Prevent a big setback from pushing too hard." I'll admit this lesson was sometimes hard to internalize. I'm a numbers guy. It would have been easy when I was healthy to think, "If I won an Olympic medal while averaging 120 miles per week, then averaging 140 per week will be that much better." What's more likely, of course, is that I would have gotten injured or overtrained and unable to run anywhere near my potential.

"Go one less mile" doesn't mean slacking off. It means knowing your limits, pushing up to the edge of them, and then having the discipline to pull back a bit. In running, you'll make more progress and get injured less often if you finish runs feeling like there's more in the tank. I never did long runs to the point of exhaustion. I never collapsed in the infield after a track workout. The people who have long, successful careers in any endeavor are those who consistently work hard but don't push themselves so much that they break down, physically or mentally. In the time when others are going the extra mile, recharge and refresh yourself so that you can be your best tomorrow.

By listening to my body rather than ignoring it, I was able to progress nicely once I resumed running. This was my only marathon for which I did no doubles (running twice a day) during my buildup. I wanted twenty-four hours of recovery between runs to lessen the chances of aggravating my quad. I focused on quality of effort and getting in key sessions, especially tempo runs and long runs, as my body allowed. In all, I had eight weeks of training, with a highest week of 116 miles, a longest tempo run of 15 miles, and a longest long run of 25 miles. That sounds like a lot, but remember, those were the longest, done only once. In an abbreviated buildup, there's no time for rest weeks; you have to keep building and building. I headed to New York City knowing I wasn't at my best yet, eager to see how I would stack up against a top field.

WHAT A PLEASANT SURPRISE!

My quad was completely recovered by race day. I wasn't concerned about reinjuring it during the race. The real issue was having only eight weeks of training. I was uncertain what I was capable of once the racing really started. On the line I thought, "I always say it's better to be undertrained than overtrained. Well, that's certainly the case today! Just go out there and try to be as competitive as possible."

It turned out that meant being pretty darn competitive. I told myself to stay under control and watch my breathing. I knew I lacked the speed and endurance to pull off any moves early on, so I was just aiming to stay with the lead group as long as possible. I felt great as we passed halfway in 1:04:56.

As was the case the year before, the first big move of the race came on First Avenue. It was almost like everyone was waiting for Hendrick Ramaala of South Africa, the defending champion, to surge there. And he did, running a 4:22 17th mile. The only ones still with him at the end of that mile were Paul Tergat of Kenya, at the time the world record holder; Robert Kipkoech Cheruiyot of Kenya, the 2003 Boston Marathon champion who would go on to win three more Boston titles; and me.

I wasn't necessarily surprised at being able to cover Hendrick's fast 17th mile, even though it was the fastest mile I'd run since before the track world championships. I still had some speed in my legs from all that 10K training earlier in the year. I was, however, concerned that I'd run that really fast mile and still had nine miles to go. Without a solid set of long runs in my buildup, I didn't know if I'd still be able to run fast at the end of the race.

Cheruiyot lost touch with us a little after 20 miles. (He and I would meet again in New York a few years later.) I did no leading. That wasn't how I usually raced, but there I was hanging on for dear life. Once there were three of us, neither Hendrick nor Paul made any big moves. Both were probably waiting for someone else to go first, or wondering why I wasn't pushing the pace, or thinking they could outsprint the others in the final stretch. Or maybe they thought all those things. I was mostly thinking, "Hang on, hang on." We entered Central Park together. I was amazed that I was still with them with only a few miles to go.

Both calves started to tighten up in the 25th mile. I had to pull back and watch Hendrick and Paul easily gap me. I changed my focus to protecting third place and getting to the finish without doing real damage to the calf.

Ahead of me, Hendrick and Paul produced the closest finish in New York City Marathon history. A furious sprint saw Paul prevail as Hendrick dove at the line, a fraction of a second behind Paul's winning time of 2:09:30. I was ecstatic as I finished third in 2:09:56, just three seconds slower than my personal best, despite being so undertrained.

GLIMPSING THE FUTURE

Coach Larsen was also ecstatic. We found each other right after the finish, and he said, "What a race! If you stay healthy, you can win this thing." Bob knew very well how unprepared I was to take on the world record holder and defending champion. Both of them had probably had perfect training heading into the marathon that year. I was extremely proud and happy to have stuck with them until the final mile.

I took to heart what Coach Larsen said. From then on I believed that, if I avoided injury and stayed healthy, I could win the New York City Marathon. I held on to that belief throughout some challenging times in the years following the 2005 race. On my darkest days I drew on that memory to remind myself how close I'd come against such great odds. I never stopped believing that even greater things were possible.

The same thing happened after the 2012 Olympic Marathon. As I'll describe in detail later, I finished fourth there despite so-so training and a very tough day at the office in the first half of the race. Before the race I had told Lewis Johnson of NBC I was 99.9 percent sure that 2012 would be my last Olympics. Afterward I thought, "I just finished fourth in the world, eight years after finishing second. I can make the 2016 Olympics. I can still win Boston. I can win New York again." If it weren't for that fourth-place finish in 2012, I wouldn't have been invited to Boston in 2014.

I didn't win New York City in 2005, and I didn't medal at the Olympics in 2012. But both were massive personal victories. Let seeing yourself succeed in tough circumstances give you hope that even greater things are possible in the future.

2006 BOSTON MARATHON

APRIL 17, 2006

PLACE **3rd**   TIME   **2:09:56**

KEY LESSON

The marathon is a metaphor for life in how it rewards patience.

During my years at UCLA, when people found out that I was a runner they'd ask what events I did. I would say, "I'm a distance runner." Then they would ask, "Have you done the Boston Marathon?" Never mind that the longest race of my life at the time was a 10K. I got the message—the average person measures your status as a runner by how you've done at the Boston Marathon.

I've already mentioned my own fascination with the event. When I got back from a trip to Eritrea in early 2003, Coach Larsen had to talk me out of hopping into that spring's marathon. The house I made an offer on in 2002 appealed to me in part because of how the hills around it would prepare me for Boston's famously up-and-down course. So I was really excited after my inspiring 2005 New York City run to turn my attention to the world's oldest and best-known marathon.

THE LEGEND OF BOSTON

People often ask me which marathon course is harder, New York City or Boston. Now that I've done both several times, I can confidently answer "Boston." In New York, the 1st mile is the longest uphill part of the course, and the 2nd mile, as you come off the Verrazano-Narrows Bridge, is the longest downhill. The opening miles are eerily quiet; there aren't spectators on the bridge. Then you start to settle into your rhythm in the 3rd mile, and you can really lock into your pace for the next several miles. In Boston, you start with a steep downhill on a narrow street, and the crowds are there almost immediately, getting you pumped up. Then you get to the 17th mile, and the Newton hills, including the legendary Heartbreak Hill, are waiting for you. If you're already fatigued by that point, you're in big trouble. In contrast, the equivalent stretch of New York has you cruising down First Avenue, which is slightly downhill and packed with the most fans along the course.

One interesting thing about the Newton hills is that when you run them in training they don't look that big. Coach Larsen and I spent two days in Boston that January. On day one, I ran the first 10 miles of the course. The next day I ran the remainder of the course. On that run, and at a moderate pace, the hills didn't seem all that different from what I ran most days in Mammoth Lakes or San Diego. Bob and I also drove the course with Bill Squires, who had coached Bill Rodgers, Greg Meyer, Dick Beardsley, and many other runners to top finishes and wins at Boston in the 1970s and 1980s. It was a great tutorial to tour the course with its foremost expert. Coach Squires would point out every little place to run the tangent or otherwise use the course to get a tactical advantage. "Meb, you're going to pull a big one for us," he told me.

I also got good pre-race advice from one of my high school

advisors, Ron Tabb. Ron placed second at the 1983 Boston Marathon with a PR of 2:09:31. He did so by overcoming a tendency to start races too fast; that year at Boston, he was the one picking off slowing runners in the second half. Ron told me that, no matter how good I felt, I shouldn't run faster than 4:50 per mile in the first half.

It can be easier to receive advice than to follow it.

RACING TO WIN

I may have been the fittest I ever was when I ran Boston that year. (I was definitely in better shape in 2006 than in 2014, when I won, which just goes to show how much of race day comes down to your mental readiness.) I had kept my good momentum going after New York City the previous November, including repeating as the national 15K champion at the Gate River Run in March. Winning Boston was both a lifetime dream and a reasonable goal, given my fitness, accomplishments, and experience. I was also now a father to our daughter Sara. Being a provider added motivation and purpose to my running.

The one experience I was missing, of course, was having raced the Boston Marathon. I'd been told Boston is tough to win in your first attempt. But I wanted to go for it. Running to win is my nature. I was fit, highly motivated, and ready to draw on experts' advice on the course.

Boston doesn't use the pacers that you'll see at many other major marathons. It's more like a championship race, where place is more important than time. But while the race organizers don't provide pacers, there's nothing keeping individual runners from engaging their own. As we set off from Hopkinton at noon on that Patriots' Day, it was obvious that that was what was happening. John Yuda of Tanzania was clearly pacing for one of his training partners, Benjamin Maiyo of Kenya. I was familiar with Maiyo. He had finished a little ahead of me when I set the U.S. record for the 10K in 2001. His last big race before Boston was finishing second, in 2:07, at the Chicago Marathon the previous October. The other guy I was watching closely was Robert Kipkoech Cheruiyot of Kenya, who had finished one place behind me at New York in November. Cheruiyot had won Boston in 2003. I always pay special attention to guys who have won big races; they know how to rise to the occasion. That's especially true on a quirky course like Boston's, which is harder to master than a flat, fast time-trial course like Chicago or London.

Yuda led Maiyo out fast. Cheruiyot went with them. After a quick chat among the three, however, Cheruiyot decided to back off the pace. One big difference between elites' and everyday runners' racing: Recreational runners can usually run their own races. You can set a time goal and do what you need to do to hit that time. You don't have to worry what the runners around you are doing (once you get past the people in the early miles who should have started behind you). Pro marathoners are usually running for a title. You can run fast times by sticking to a time schedule, and you'll usually move up in the last 10K to get a decent finishing place. But you're almost never going to win by ignoring your competitors. To win races at the highest level, you're always responding to or initiating moves that whittle down the pack until one runner is left in front. So when Maiyo and Cheruiyot followed Yuda to a fast early pace, I had to go with them if I wanted to fight for a victory.

What I didn't have to do was help push the pace. That was my mistake in my first Boston. It's the same mistake so many people make there. You feel so good, and the first half is primarily flat or downhill, and the crowds are amazing, and it's the Boston Marathon, and . . . well, it's easy to get carried away.

OOPS! NOW WHAT?

The display on the watch I used in those days made you choose between total running time or per-mile split time. I was using the latter. For most of the opening half of the race I would hit the watch at a mile marker and see that we were going faster than 4:50 per mile, the pace that Ron Tabb had told me not to exceed. Have I mentioned how good I felt?

So it wasn't until we reached the halfway point that I saw our total running time. We hit the 13.1-mile mark in 1:02:43, or mid 2:05 marathon pace. The Boston course record at the time was 2:07:15. The world record was 2:04:55. My personal best was 2:09:53. I thought, "Well, I didn't listen to Ron's advice. I can't do anything about what I've done the last 13.1 miles. It's either going to be a great day where I cut two or three minutes off my PR, or it's going to be a long day. Be ready for either."

It was the latter. When we hit the Newton hills, I hit the Wall. Cheruiyot passed me in the 18th mile. Maiyo was way ahead of me. I was alone in third place, struggling to get through the hardest part of the course on legs that were shot from the classic Boston unforced error—too fast too soon. In any marathon, but especially at Boston, for every seeming advantage you gain in the early miles by running too fast, you pay back with interest over the final miles.

Boston 2006 was the first time I wore a USA jersey in a non-Olympic marathon. The idea came from the race organizers, who wanted to help fans and spectators better identify the top runners. Around that time it also became common for elites' bibs to show their name rather than a number. That little uniform tweak got me through the closing miles. The crowd kept cheering "Go, Meb!" or "USA! USA!" I drew energy from that and was able to hold on for third place despite having to dig really deep to keep going. Up ahead, Cheruiyot passed Maiyo and won in 2:07:14, one second under the old course record. I took a little satisfaction in contributing to the record being broken.

I took more satisfaction from my time of 2:09:56. It was the same time I'd run in New York the previous fall. It was only three seconds slower than my personal best. Of the seven marathons I'd run at that point, two were championship races, where time doesn't matter. In the other five, I'd run between 2:09:53 and 2:10:03 in four of them. If you race frequently, at any level, you should be able to be just as consistent. If you put in the work and stay healthy, you're the same person from one race to the next. Sure, there will be variations because of weather or tough courses or an off day. But overall, in running and life, most of your performances should be in the thick part of the bell curve. I'm very proud to have retired from competitive running with the most sub-2:10 marathons—nine—of any American. The average time of the twenty-five marathons I finished was 2:12:52. Those stats show that I regularly produced when it mattered, which was made possible by diligent preparation.

LESSON LEARNED, BIG-TIME

I never had a bad race. My results weren't always what I wanted, but each was a learning experience—for racing and life. You usually learn more from setbacks, such as being aggressive too early in a marathon, than from once-in-a-lifetime days.

After finishing third despite making a huge error, I knew how I could win Boston. For starters, don't run the first half in 1:02! I learned the hard way that no matter how great you feel early on, you have to save something for the hills. It's one thing to prepare for them in training. I had done so with tempo runs that started with downhill miles and ended with climbing. It's another thing to have the patience to be able to put that preparation to use. I had squandered that opportunity in my first Boston. Rather than beat up on myself, I filed that lesson away. I never stopped believing that one day I'd have a chance to implement it.

One way the marathon is different from other races is that its lessons often have parallels in the rest of life. The patience needed to master the marathon is a transferable skill. Taking the long view, putting in the unglamorous daily work, finding joy in the process, saving something for the inevitable challenges— these traits have helped me be a better husband, father, brother, and friend. The greatest rewards I've felt from all those roles in my life have come over the long term, not through immediate payoff.

I left Boston that spring convinced I could someday win there. I already felt that way about New York City. When I returned to New York in the fall, my patience was tested like it never had been in a marathon.

8

2006 NEW YORK CITY MARATHON

NOVEMBER 5, 2006

PLACE **20th**   TIME   **2:22:02**

KEY LESSON

Do what you can to minimize exposure to risks, but also accept that some things are out of your control.

Here's one hint that you're not going to win the New York City Marathon: You've just stepped out of a Porta-Potty for the third time in the last few miles.

That's one "lesson" I learned at the 2006 New York City Marathon. It was my first truly disappointing marathon. In a race I felt primed to win, I wound up running almost 10 minutes slower than ever, and finishing twentieth, not first.

The real lesson from a weekend that involved lost luggage and food poisoning: Always be mindful of Murphy's Law while maintaining perspective on what you can and can't control. This lesson is definitely as important in all parts of life as it is in running.

NOT OFF TO A GREAT START

Since winning Olympic silver, I'd placed second and third at New York City and third at Boston. As I noted in the previous chapter, my times in those three races were all between 2:09:53 and 2:09:56. That time is often good enough to win either race. So as I began my buildup for the 2006 edition of New York, I liked my chances. At that point in my career I was thinking this marathon thing that people had long told me was my destiny was becoming a reality.

There was a little added urgency to New York that year. The following year, the 2008 Olympic Marathon Trials would be run the day before the New York City Marathon. (Yup, the 2008 trials would be run in 2007.) I would be running that race to try to make my third Olympic team. If I made the team, then I'd be running the Olympic Marathon in late August 2008. I'd done well with that quick turnaround between the 2004 Olympics and that year's New York, but there was no guarantee I could pull it off again. And I was thirty-one years old, what many people think is around a marathoner's peak age, for the 2006 race.

Four weeks before the marathon I ran the San Jose Rock 'n' Roll Half Marathon. Or I should say I ran most of it. I wound up dropping out of the race, my first go at the distance, when I went there hoping to break the American record. Maybe I should have seen this as an omen.

The weekend began with a long drive from Mammoth Lakes to San Jose made longer by a snowstorm and a closed road in Yosemite National Park. My goal was to break Mark Curp's U.S. record of 60:55, despite having put in 121 miles the week before. That plan went out the window when Duncan Kibet of Kenya, at the time the second-fastest marathoner in the world, was a late entrant. He took off like a bat out of hell, and I went with him. I was under American record pace through 10 miles, but then my right hamstring cramped in the 11th mile. I reluctantly stepped off the course, so as not to risk more serious injury. It was only the second race of my life I didn't finish. After another eight-hour drive home, my hamstring hurt even more. I took a few days off from running and hoped for the best. The leg improved and I resumed full training, only to catch the flu a week and a half before New York. And then the fun really started.

TRAVELING A LITTLE TOO LIGHTLY

My trip to New York on the Wednesday before Sunday's marathon was the first time Yordanos and I flew to a race with our first daughter, Sara, who was eight months old. As new parents we were suddenly traveling with lots of additional items (strollers, diapers, wipes, etc.). We needed all the space we could get in the overhead bins and under our seats. We had a direct flight from San Diego to New York, so for the first time since college, I checked my running gear. What could go wrong?

Well, for starters, it turns out that your luggage can get lost even if you have a direct flight! You can imagine my confusion when we landed and didn't see my luggage on the baggage carousel. We were told not to worry, the bag would be delivered to our hotel in twenty-four hours. Then we were told forty-eight hours. It never arrived. (I later learned the bag never got loaded in San Diego.)

So suddenly, before a race I was hoping to win, I had no training shoes, racing flats, race-day uniform, socks, massage stick, and so on. I was sponsored by Nike at the time and was able to get replacements for most items at Niketown in Manhattan. The racing flats had to be shipped to me from elsewhere. They were my usual models, but when I laced them up on race morning, it was the first time I'd run in them. That's not ideal—you never know if a particular pair of shoes, even a model you're used to, is going to agree with you until you run in them. As it turned out, something else even more significant disagreed with me before the race.

WHAT ELSE CAN GO WRONG?

On the Thursday before the race, I had dinner with a large group at a hotel restaurant. I ordered chicken fettuccini. I'd always figured you can't go wrong with chicken.

You can. A few hours later I was in the bathroom for the first of many times that evening, dealing with the effects of food poisoning. I just couldn't believe this was happening, especially after so much other bad luck.

Again, as a professional athlete subject to regular drug testing, I always tried to be careful about what I took when I got sick. You can't be sure of everything that's in medication, and you don't want to find out after the fact that the over-the-counter medicine you bought in a panic contains a banned substance. My default was to not take medication unless I had an infection, and to rest until the illness was out of my system. So I decided to let the food poisoning run its course. I let the race organizers know what I was dealing with, but I never seriously considered not starting the marathon. Four weeks earlier I'd been on American record pace in the half marathon for more than 10 miles. Sure, I'd had some mishaps since, but I still felt it was my year to win New York.

I thought the race would come down to defending champion Paul Tergat of Kenya; the 2004 champion, Hendrick Ramaala of South Africa; and me, just like it had the year before. I was also keeping an eye on Hailu Negussie of Ethiopia, who had won Boston in 2005, and Stefano Baldini of Italy, who had run so impressively to win the Olympic Marathon in 2004. On race morning, I was confident in my preparation but nervous about the events of the past few days. Would I have enough energy to race hard for 26.2 miles? My cause was helped by a conservative early pace. I was tucked in the lead pack past halfway and liking my chances.

But a little before we hit First Avenue in Manhattan, when the first real moves of the race are usually made, I started losing contact with the leaders. By the time I was on First Avenue, I was really struggling. I made a pit stop. I resumed running. I made another pit stop. I resumed running. And so on. In all, I had to make five pit stops. I had hit the Wall in my first marathon, but this was the first time I experienced such a struggle so far from the finish. I had thoughts like, "Wow, I can't believe I still have eight miles to go." The situation was made that much worse because all summer and fall I'd been thinking it was my time to win.

Adding to the struggle of those last miles: It was the first time I didn't know what position I was in. It has always been important to me to fight for every place. But when you duck into a Porta-Potty five times, you have no idea how many people have passed you. Was I in twentieth place? Thirtieth? Fiftieth?

And then there was the fact that Lance Armstrong was running. There was a lot of hype before the race that the now-disgraced cycling champion would run a world-class marathon time. I certainly didn't think Lance was going to run 2:10, but could he run around 2:20? It didn't seem impossible on the face of it. Every time I made a pit stop, I wondered, "Did Lance just pass me? Am I going to get beaten by a cyclist?!" (I wasn't. Armstrong finished 869th in 2:59:36.)

I finally staggered across the finish line, hungry and dehydrated, in 2:22:02, close to 10 minutes slower than I'd run on the same course in my first marathon. My finishing place of twentieth was also by far the worst I'd placed in a marathon.

I had, predictably, a blister from racing in the too-new shoes. But what really stung was learning that Marilson Gomes dos Santos of Brazil had won in 2:09:57, by making a late-race move that the field didn't try to cover until he was too far ahead. His time was right in that narrow range I'd run in my last few marathons. I could easily imagine a scenario where he and I broke away, the pack let us go, and then I used my knowledge of the course to claim victory. Part of me thought, "It's so hard to win the New York City Marathon. My chance has passed."

THE HELPFUL VIEW OF MURPHY'S LAW

Murphy's Law is usually stated as some version of "If something can go wrong, it will." Most people take that to mean the universe is out to get them, so what does it matter what you do? I'll admit I felt like that after setback upon setback before and during the New York City Marathon that year.

The better way to think about Murphy's Law is how the colleagues of Edward Murphy, an aerospace engineer, came to understand it. They took the view that before something like testing a rocket, they should consider everything that could go wrong and then take steps to minimize the chance of those things happening. One (now) obvious example: The airline might lose your luggage. So prioritize your carry-ons to include what you absolutely need, which, if you're traveling to a race, includes your running shoes and racing outfit. In fact, I've become someone who doesn't check luggage, and not because of the fees. Even if I'm going on a two-week trip, I carry everything with me. (If nothing else, I'm now a very efficient packer.)

Throughout the rest of my career I also tried to be more careful about food. I started packing more of my own trusted items, both those of sponsors like Krave Jerky and Generation UCAN, and packaged foods such as nuts, almond butter, and raw honey. I also often brought homemade bread to big races. Doing so anticipates and solves not only the potential risk of exposure to contaminated food but also that of finding myself without high-quality food when I'm about to ask my body for a peak performance.

Another way I implemented Murphy's Law was to start always carrying hand sanitizer, especially after I (finally!) won New York in 2009. I love meeting people and making appearances, but a lot of travel and handshakes means more risk of exposure to germs. I got sick soon after my New York win and from then on, took to heart messages about the transmission of germs. I now always travel with a pocket-size vial of hand sanitizer I can refill from bigger bottles or the stations in hotel lobbies and offices.

These are just a few examples of how I put Murphy's Law to work to meet my situation. You can probably think of common scenarios in your running and life where anticipating potential pitfalls can lessen the chance of them happening. Maybe you live where the roads are treacherous in the winter, so you run on the treadmill or put underfoot stabilizers on your shoes. Maybe you get sick whenever anyone at work comes down with a cold, so you ask about working from home in the few days before a big race. This approach isn't about being obsessive-compulsive. It's just rigorously applying common sense so that things you can control don't keep you from reaching your goals.

ON NOT BEING A CONTROL FREAK

You've probably realized by now that I'm meticulous about preparation. That's always been the case, whether the task at hand is school, marathoning, parenting, investing, public speaking, or pretty much anything else. I'm also a planner—I like to know what I'm going to be doing when.

Yet during my career, I often appeared to my competitors as being laid-back. Take the special bus rides we'd get to the start of the Boston and New York City marathons. I'd overhear talk about how challenging the weather was going to be or concerns that the bus was running later than advertised. At that point, thinking about those things is wasted energy. There's nothing you can do to change them. Of course in those situations I would have preferred better weather or more timely transportation. But the thing to do in a situation like that is to concentrate on what you can control, such as staying on top of your hydration if it's hot or prioritizing the parts of your warm-up if you're running late.

This mind-set combines the lessons of Murphy's Law and the serenity prayer, which is about accepting what you can't change, working on what you can change, and having the wisdom to know the difference. The unexpected is always a possibility; that's why it's called *unexpected*. In any endeavor, focusing on the things you can control provides guidance on how to proceed and peace of mind that you've done what you can to succeed. Getting waylaid when I thought I could win New York in 2006 tested my faith in that outlook. Once I got past the immediate heartbreak, however, I was at peace with the outcome.

Then came perhaps the most trying year of my career.

2007 LONDON MARATHON

APRIL 22, 2007

PLACE AND TIME   **did not finish**

KEY LESSON

Sometimes it's better to cut your losses than stick it out.

A s runners, nothing we do happens in isolation. We train hard this week to be faster next week. We're wiser today because of learning from past mistakes. And sometimes, what happens during moments of triumph leads to setbacks much later on.

My run at the 2007 London Marathon—the only marathon I dropped out of—was an example of a great day setting up a bad day. I remain convinced, however, that not finishing that marathon was the right choice, and that my doing so turned out to be a good example of knowing when to call it a day.

A BLISTERING PACE

My main goal in 2007 was to make my third Olympic team at the Olympic Marathon Trials, which would be run in November on the day before the New York City Marathon. That race in hilly Central Park would be all about placing in the top three; time wouldn't matter. I also wanted to improve my personal best in the marathon. The best time and place for that would be April in London, a flat, fast course where men's and women's world records have been set.

I started the year by placing third at the national half marathon championship. In that mid-January race in Houston, my Mammoth Track Club teammate Ryan Hall ran 59:43 to shatter the American record. Ryan would be making his marathon debut in London. I was elated for what he accomplished in Houston, but also was eager to see how we would match up when it really counted in London. Six weeks before the marathon, I defeated Ryan and other top Americans at the Gate River Run 15K in Jacksonville, Florida. I left Gate River satisfied with my sixth win there and the feeling that I was on the right track heading into London.

Unfortunately, I also left with a blister on the ball of my left foot. This wasn't your run-of-the-mill running blister—it was the size of a golf ball. Two days after the race, back home in Mammoth Lakes, it became so painful I needed to go to the hospital to have it drained. My car wouldn't start, so my teammate Deena Kastor, who had won the women's race at Gate River, picked me up. She couldn't believe it when the national 15K champion hauled himself out to her car using a broom as a crutch. When draining the blister didn't really help, it was removed, resulting in a half-inch gash in the bottom of my foot.

This problem with my foot was more a wound than an injury. It remained an issue for the rest of my professional running career. With the exception of my final 26.2-miler, I reinjured the wound in every marathon I ran from 2007 onward. After a marathon, I could count on the area to be raw and require care and caution so that it didn't get infected. If you ever saw me limping in the days after a marathon, it was almost certainly because the race had aggravated the wound.

The wound was even more troublesome right after I suffered it. Running was out of the question. So was simulating running in the pool, because the wound might get infected. I could cycle without aggravating the wound if I wore a Dr. Scholl's pad. I rode twice a day, for up to three hours at a time. There was do-or-die pressure to stay in good shape and get to the starting line healthy. I was able to resume running in late March, including some short tempo runs and a good long run. Going into London I felt like I was still ready to run fast. I'd done a decent job of maintaining the great fitness I'd built before Gate River.

A TOUGH DECISION

Everything was perfect in the early miles of the London Marathon. Ryan and I ran together, just off the lead pack. It was great for us two teammates to be there helping and encouraging each other in one of the world's top marathons. It was rare during my career to run alongside an American in an international marathon; two other notable times were with Alan Culpepper in the 2004 Olympics and Josphat Boit at Boston in 2014. I went through halfway on pace to run right around 2:09:00, which would be a personal best by almost a minute.

Then things went awry. I'd been running under 5:00 per mile, but suddenly my 14th mile was a 5:21. My 15th was a 5:28. The leaders were getting pretty far away from me, and my goal of a PR was quickly slipping away.

More important, I was running these slower times despite feeling like I was working just as hard as when I was running much faster just a few miles earlier. When that happens so early in a marathon, it usually means something is off mechanically—

because you're not running as efficiently, the same effort level results in running slower. In this case, my right Achilles tendon was becoming increasingly bothersome. I was compensating for the still-tender wound in my left foot by shifting more of the work to my right leg.

I could have kept running with that level of pain. But a serious Achilles tendon injury can be career-ending, whether because of running on it so long that it tears or doing enough damage to require surgery. I was especially mindful of those risks with the Olympic Trials and, I hoped, the Olympics coming up. I decided I couldn't justify jeopardizing the rest of my career and, more immediately, the 2008 Olympics, just for the sake of finishing London with a really bad time. I stepped off the course in the 16th mile. (Ryan went on to place 7th in 2:08:24, the fastest marathon debut by an American.)

Dropping out of the London Marathon was one of the hardest on-the-go decisions I made during my career. Everything in my nature and my upbringing encourages enduring present difficulties to achieve more in the future. This was only the third DNF result in all my years of running, and my first in a marathon. Even more so than in shorter races, part of the marathon's mythology is finishing what you start, no matter what. There were also professional consequences to consider: Would I ever be welcomed back at London after dropping out my first time there? A clause in my Nike contract meant that my base pay might be reduced. Despite all of those counterarguments, I was at peace with my decision to drop out, for reasons I'll get to in a bit.

What I needed to get to immediately after dropping out was the finish line. My race number gave me free entry to the London Underground. I sat down in a train, with my head down, very much aware of the bib reading "MEB" pinned to the USA jersey I had on. My pity party didn't last long. A recreational runner who had dropped out told me that Haile Gebrselassie, one of my heroes and one of the greatest runners in history, was on the train, having also dropped out. Then Stefano Baldini, the 2004 Olympic champion, got on, another DNF. When we got off the train near the race headquarters hotel, we saw American Khalid Khannouchi, a former London winner and world record holder, who had also dropped out. Most people figured we had finished, and some started congratulating us. (The short answer about how to handle that situation is to say "thank you" and keep moving forward.)

WHEN IT'S TIME TO CUT YOUR LOSSES

After London, I never dropped out of another race. Maybe it will help you to hear that I most definitely thought about dropping out of every marathon I ran, even when I won Boston in 2014. There's a point in every marathon where you think, "Why am I doing this?!" As I'll describe later, I was *this* close to dropping out of the 2012 Olympic Marathon, and nobody would have criticized me for dropping out of the 2013 New York City Marathon, when I suddenly couldn't lift my leg with seven miles still to run.

We runners pride ourselves on our perseverance. We see things through despite pain and fatigue. Usually sticking it out is the right choice—those negative feelings are almost always temporary sensations along the road to meeting our goals. Getting past those bad patches makes our accomplishments that much sweeter.

But there are times when ending things early is the best choice. In running, if you have a big injury pop up out of nowhere, something is seriously wrong with your body. Continuing to run will make the injury worse and could cost you untold

amounts of time off later. It could perhaps end your running career. The same is true of an ache or pain that causes you to limp
or otherwise alter your running form. Continuing to run in that
situation could not only worsen the original injury that changed
how you run but also lead to injury elsewhere as you compen-
sate for that initial injury. That was my situation in London—I
was at risk of doing severe damage to my right Achilles tendon,
which was strained because of how I was compensating for the
wound on my left foot. Knowing when to cut your losses isn't
wimping out. It's making the rational choice if you've properly
calculated the costs and benefits.

That doesn't mean it's not difficult. When you've invested a
lot of time, money, and/or effort into something, it can be hard
to pull out of that endeavor even when doing so is the most
rational choice. Economists call this the sunk-cost fallacy: You
base your decision about the future in part on costs you've in-
curred and can't get back. For example, you buy a movie ticket
and are reluctant to leave before the movie is over, even though
you hate the movie; exiting early feels like you're wasting the
money you spent on the ticket. In running, you might think, "I
can't drop out of this marathon, even though staying in it will
probably result in long-term injury, because then all my training will be wasted." In both cases, your "costs" (the price of the
movie ticket, the many hours spent training) are past expen-
ditures. If what you spent them on isn't going to end well, continuing that undertaking stems from your emotional attachment
to those costs, not logic.

Again, I'm not advocating quitting when things get tough.
As I explained earlier in this book, "run to win" means running
to get the best out of yourself. Usually that means overcoming
short- and long-term challenges. But when things are clearly
heading the wrong way, when continuing is obviously going to

lead to long-term negative consequences, you need to have the wisdom to stop. That's true in marathoning, that's true in relationships, that's true in business. Know when to cut your losses and move on to better things.

As I got older, I got better about applying this lesson to my training. For example, there were days when I planned to do an interval workout but just didn't feel right while warming up, and I postponed the workout. I've also cut easy runs short based on how I felt. (Sure enough, sometimes the following day I came down with a cold.) Toward the end of my career I took more spontaneous days off from running, when I just wasn't feeling well. I sensed that training that day would harm rather than increase my fitness a week later.

Obviously you have to know yourself well to be confident that you're making the right decision in these cases, where there's not the dramatic evidence like an injury that's throwing off your running form. You don't want to get in the habit of quitting or putting things off just because you don't feel like doing the task at hand. Most runners, however, are strong-willed, and more often do what they planned to do regardless of how things are going. If you're honest with yourself, you know when your body and mind aren't on the same page. That's when it's time to save it for another day.

After London, the first order of business was to let my foot and Achilles tendon heal. They did so pretty quickly, and I had a great summer of racing on the roads and track. That was more evidence that I'd made the right choice to drop out of London. My fitness and confidence were high heading into the Olympic Marathon Trials that November. I had good reason to think I could get my first marathon win. I had no reason to think I was about to be tested as never before.

KEY LESSON

You're not always going to get what you think you deserve. These trials can help you realize what's really important.

Halfway into the 2008 Olympic Marathon Trials, my right calf started feeling a little tight. This development was worrisome but not entirely surprising. I had taken a few days off from running during my buildup to the Trials because of the calf, out of caution, not necessity. I was probably fitter than I'd ever been—more so than when I won an Olympic medal and the New York City and Boston Marathons—and believed I had a great shot at my first marathon win. Heading into my tenth marathon, I had enough experience to know I could afford a few rest days for the sake of not jeopardizing my chances.

A little calf niggle here and there is the sort of thing you expect when you're pushing your body to its limits. By this point in my marathon career I had plenty of experience in finessing my way through minor aches and pains (and worse!) to show up ready to race. When my calf started to tighten in the Trials, I didn't panic. I figured it would be a brief bad patch en route to victory.

Ten minutes later, I knew otherwise. The calf tightness was the harbinger of a major injury, one that would keep me off the Olympic team and that would ultimately test my very future in running. As it turned out, that injury wasn't even the worst thing that happened that day.

NOT THE TRIAL I WAS EXPECTING

The 2008 Trials were held in November 2007, one day before the New York City Marathon. Rather than the famous five-borough course, we started on Fifth Avenue and ran through Times Square to Central Park, where we did five roughly 5-mile loops of the park. Central Park is famous for its rolling hills. Some people said the Trials course was so hard the race would be won in 2:15, minutes slower than usual. I doubted the race would be that slow. Still, I thought the course played to my strengths. I had raced several times in Central Park, I was used to much bigger hills in Mammoth Lakes and San Diego, and the hills would reward being a good tactical racer more than a flat, fast course would.

When I visualized how the race would play out, I most often saw myself battling my teammate Ryan Hall for the win over the last few miles. Ryan had the fastest qualifying time, from his great debut at London in April. I was eager to duel with Ryan—not because of something like wanting to put him in his place or show him who's boss; that's not what competition is to me. Mutual respect and lack of animosity is what underlies true competition. I felt like Ryan and I would bring out the best in each other. Ryan felt the same way. When we left Mammoth Lakes for New York, he said, "I just want to be on that flight with you," meaning the flight to Beijing for the Olympics. Both of us wanted the other to finish in the top three, the placing needed to make the team.

So it was fitting that Ryan and I ran next to each other amid a huge pack in New York. The early miles were uneventful, except for one thing that seemed odd at the time and would turn out to be monumental. During the second loop of Central Park, around the 10-mile mark, an ambulance came onto the course. I said to Ryan, "Why can't they keep the course closed? Don't they have access somewhere else?" By this time there were five of us in the lead pack. I suggested to Ryan we push the pace to try to get the lead pack down to three. Ryan asked, "Isn't it too early?" I said no. He said, "Let's see what the next mile split is." When we saw that we'd run just under 4:50 for that mile, I said, "That's fine." That pace would eventually take its toll on others. Ryan and I, the two favorites, could just sit tight, I thought.

Ryan soon thought otherwise. He began pushing in the 13th mile. My calf had just started to bother me. I knew Ryan was in phenomenal shape and would try to run hard to the finish. I had to go with him if I wanted to win.

That dream of my first marathon victory disappeared in the next 10 minutes. Ryan kept hammering. Suddenly my right hip started hurting. My mind was saying, "Cover the move, cover the move," but my legs weren't responding. Change of plans: Instead of winning, I would finish second, as I had in the 2004 Trials. But Dathan Ritzenhein, who, like Ryan, was running only his second marathon, went after Ryan. Now I was in third. My goal became to finish in the top three. Third is as good as first, I told myself; the important thing is to make the team. Then Dan Browne, a 2004 Olympic Marathon teammate, sprinted really hard past me. I couldn't do anything about it. Now I was in fourth. That's the alternate spot—if one of the top three are unable to run the Olympics, or make the team in the 10K and opt out of the marathon, the alternate gets to race. That became my goal. But then came former world record holder Khalid Khannouchi. When Brian Sell, who would eventually finish third behind Ryan and Dathan, flew by me, I knew that being the alternate wasn't going to happen. My goal shifted to finishing, despite the excruciating pain in my hip.

The last person to pass me was Nate Jenkins. He's a big guy, 40 pounds heavier than me, who I could hear coming from 100 meters away. Like me, Nate is a student of the sport, so he'll know I mean no disrespect in relaying that I thought, "God, please help me beat this guy." Nate is an incredibly hard worker who was having the race of his life, but still, I was an Olympic silver medalist who regularly took on the best runners in the world. Nate was probably at least as surprised as I was that we were in a late-race battle for 7th place. I pushed so hard to try to beat Nate, but I could only watch as he worked his way past me. Soon after, someone in the crowd yelled, "Meb, we love you! New York loves you! You're still our hero!" I started crying. I had given 110 percent in training and racing but was watching in slow motion as my dream of returning to the Olympics had become a nightmare.

A MUCH GREATER LOSS

I finished eighth in 2:15:09, more than six minutes behind Ryan's Olympic Trials record of 2:09:02. I collapsed to the ground. A former training partner came over to help me up and said,

"Did you hear about Ryan?" I thought he meant Ryan Hall. It was obvious from earlier in the race he was going to win. So I thought maybe something unusual had happened at the finish. I asked, "What, did he fall?" "No, Ryan Shay," my friend replied. "He died."

The ambulance we'd seen on the course was for Ryan Shay, a friend and training partner. He had suffered cardiac arrest in the 6th mile and collapsed; he was pronounced dead when the ambulance got him to Lenox Hill Hospital. Ryan had been born with an enlarged heart that put him at a small risk for such a scenario.

I didn't know those details when I learned Ryan was dead. I just knew that a great young man was suddenly lost. Ryan and I had shared many miles and meals together. Just that morning, I had sat next to him and we had talked about how cool it was to feel like we had midtown Manhattan to ourselves as we were bused to the start line. After our brief chat, we had gotten back to our respective pre-race rituals. To hear just a few hours later that Ryan was dead was stunning. How can that happen? It's still striking to think about today, more than a decade later.

Things got even weirder at the post-race press conference. We were told by race organizers not to discuss Ryan's death, even though most of the media covering the race had heard the news.

Some people took things I said after the race to mean I thought that, as the reigning Olympic silver medalist, I was above the U.S. system. So let me be clear: I didn't mean that USA Track & Field, the governing body of the sport in the United States, should have named me to the team. The U.S. system—one race on one day, with the top three making the team—is the fairest. No athlete wants to have their Olympic chances decided by a committee or some other subjective system. Even if the people picking the team have the best of intentions, there will be at least the appearance of favoritism. (In some countries, it's much worse, with clear cases of payoffs and grudges determining who gets named to a team.) Where I'd like to see a change is in the Olympic system, not the U.S. selection system. I think the three medalists from the previous Olympic Marathon should be granted automatic entry to the next one. That would add only three people per marathon; there would be plenty of room on the roads to accommodate them. This small tweak is similar to what happens at the World Championships, where the defending champion in each event gets automatic entry.

The rest of the day was a blur. The severe pain I was in and my disappointment about not making the Olympic team didn't seem all that important in light of Ryan Shay's death. I asked my brother Hawi to find Ryan's wife, Alicia, but she had already checked out.

The next day should have been a time of celebration, of taking in the New York City Marathon while honoring three Olympians (ideally, including me). Instead, Ryan Shay was dead, and I couldn't walk. I had to crawl on my knees and elbows to get around the hotel room. Yordanos was at least as distraught as me. She said, "This is not the way I want to see you live. You have your UCLA degree, I have my college degree, we have other ways of making a living." I was taking an ice bath when I called Josh Cox, a friend of Ryan's and mine who had run the Trials. We discussed all that had happened in the race and tried to support each other through our shared faith.

By that Monday I started accepting that something other than the usual post-marathon soreness was going on. For the past two nights, if I wanted to shift while sleeping, I had to lift my leg with my arms to turn onto my other side. When Coach Larsen left my room, he said, "You put it out there, you did the best you could. It's been a great pleasure working with you." I thought, "What does this mean? Is my career over?"

PUTTING THINGS IN PERSPECTIVE

The following weeks were some of my most difficult as an adult. It was hard to know what to think about all that had happened on race morning. I had worked so hard to prepare for what I thought I deserved, my first marathon victory. I was broken, physically and emotionally. Whenever I got too caught up in my situation, Ryan Shay's death would come to mind, and I'd be sent reeling.

I had seen a doctor two days after the marathon and told him I thought I needed an MRI. He had said I didn't need one, that my body was just beat up from a tough course. I should have been more insistent. I wound up not running for six weeks after the Trials. I couldn't even walk normally. I spent a lot of time stretching, using a foam roller, going at my glutes with a softball, anything to try to get my body to come around. That self-treatment helped me feel a little looser for a little while, but the underlying issue of hip pain and stiffness remained.

Before leaving New York, Yordanos and I talked a lot and prayed a lot. I believe that things happen for a reason. We prayed that if it was God's will that my running career end, let it be. I was happy with an Olympic medal, an American record, and several national titles on the road and track and in cross-country. Trying to look at the big picture can be hard. Sometimes I did better than others at accepting that no matter how strongly I felt I deserved anything in life, God can have other plans.

Over the holidays I talked with some of my brothers. I told them I was thinking about retiring from running and that I needed their support more than ever. Their love reminded me that, if you're fortunate, there will always be people in your life who value you for who you are at your core, regardless of what you've achieved. Ryan Shay's death remained on my mind while I pondered my future. Whether I might or might not set another personal record in the marathon seemed inconsequential in comparison. And yet . . .

Deep down I knew that at the Trials I'd had a bad day. I'd had a *really* bad day. But in my prayers and thoughts, I kept coming back to one idea: I hadn't yet tapped all of my God-given talent. I had been in the best shape of my life trying for my first marathon win. Something had gone wrong with my body in the process, but it didn't feel like the definitive end. I knew that other top runners had come back from horrible injuries to peak performances. I still had the drive, I still loved working hard, I still loved running as a way to inspire myself and others to strive for our best. I felt that the answer to my prayers was to try to come back stronger than ever.

KEY LESSON

Celebrate every personal best and see each as a link to an even better future.

My resolve after the Olympic Trials to return to the top of the running world hit a significant snag almost immediately. My body was still broken. The year 2008, which I had hoped would include my third time at the Olympics, was instead a one-step-forward, two-steps-back trial. I probably spent more time rehabbing my body than running. I quietly withdrew well before the start of the New York City Marathon. I was fit enough to finish in the top ten, but not to challenge for the victory against the stacked field. It was the only year of my professional career when I didn't run a marathon since my debut at the distance in 2002.

But rather than be defeated by what felt like setback after setback, I emerged from 2008 stronger than ever. It was a long, long road to the London Marathon in April 2009. There, I learned never to take a personal record for granted. I also relearned how to see personal records as pointers toward even greater things, rather than accepting them as ultimate achievements. My run in London and all that preceded it set me up for the greatest part of my career.

REBUILDING MY BODY, PART 1

I resumed running six weeks after the Olympic Marathon Trials, in the second half of December 2007. It didn't go well. If I was running down a street and wanted to get to the sidewalk, I had to wait until there was a ramp. I didn't have the power or lift to just hop up on the curb. It was odd, and scary, to be an Olympic medalist who looked for ADA-accessible routes on his runs.

Of course, that didn't stop me from quickly getting back to running ten to fifteen miles a day. But even without the sidewalk issue, I knew something was still wrong. My efficient, smooth running form had always been one of my strengths. Now I felt like I was listing to the right. Running was like continually righting an out-of-alignment car to keep it going in a straight line.

In January I saw a Los Angeles doctor who said I had an abdominal tear he wanted to operate on. Yordanos told me, "No way are you going under the knife without a second opinion." So I flew to Phoenix with my high school mentor, Dr. Steve Van Camp, to see a highly respected sports medicine doctor, Lewis Maharam, who was in Arizona working at a race. He said he thought I had piriformis syndrome, a glute muscle problem, that could be relieved with a cortisone shot. To see where exactly to give the shot, Dr. Maharam ordered an MRI. That needed to take place in New York City, where his office was, so I made another trip.

When the imaging came back, Dr. Maharam said, "The good news is, you don't need a cortisone shot or surgery. The bad news is that you had a pelvic stress fracture ten weeks ago and it's finally starting to heal." No wonder I couldn't run normally!

A month later, another MRI showed that the stress fracture had barely improved. It was time for drastic measures. I pulled out of April's London Marathon. My focus became making the 10K team at the Olympic Track Trials in July. I stopped listening to doctors' advice and trusted my instincts. In the short term, that meant not running, and not even cycling. I needed as little impact as possible to let the stress fracture heal. Every day I drove twenty miles to water-run in a pool. If you've ever done even a short bout of water running, you know how monotonous it can be. On the positive side, I made many friends among the older folks there doing water aerobics. Some even sent me a card after I won New York City in 2009.

By the Olympic Track Trials in July, I was healthy but behind on race fitness. I finished 13th. I would be watching the Beijing Olympics from home. Still, I was on the right track. In August, I finished second in a fast time at the Falmouth Road Race, a 7-miler on Cape Cod. In early September I went to the Memorial Van Damme track meet in Brussels, Belgium, the site of many distance world records over the years. I felt ready to get my American 10K record under 27:00.

REBUILDING MY BODY, PART 2

In Brussels, it was my body, not the American record, that got broken. Things were going great in the race when I suddenly had no lift. My pace slowed by several seconds per 400-meter lap despite my working just as hard. I placed 16th out of 18 finishers and was lapped by four runners. I left Brussels with an injury to my left tensor fascia latae (TFL), a hip extensor muscle in the upper front of the leg.

I went to the Olympic Training Center in Colorado Springs for intensive therapy. What I thought was going to be a week-long trip turned into a month-and-a-half stay. Exercise physiologist Krista Austin guided my treatment, which most days lasted for ten to twelve hours. The team at the training center put together a personalized program that helped my TFL recover and gave me the foundational strength and mobility to keep those biomechanical issues from recurring.

Mammoth Track Club coach Terrence Mahon connected with the conditioning guru Dan Pfaff, who helped me immensely. One of the most important things I learned from him was a series of running form drills. For the rest of my career, I did these drills post-run almost every day. These drills keep my running form fluid and my body balanced. They were key to being able to run at a top level from my midthirties into my early forties, when I retired from professional racing. Even now, as a recreational runner, I still do them most days.

Thanks to the extensive therapy, I was able to resume good training while in Colorado Springs. Nonetheless, I made the difficult decision to pull out of November's New York City Marathon. As with the track trials, I didn't have enough time to build the fitness needed to be competitive. I didn't want to run New York unless I felt I could battle for the win or a podium spot. At the end of the Olympic year of 2008, it might have looked like my career was on the decline. Who else but an increasingly fragile, aging runner would see close to fifty doctors in one year, as I had? I knew otherwise.

BACK TO HEALTH, BACK TO LONDON

Consistency is the key to running your best. By bypassing New York, I was able to keep my momentum going and string together a solid block of training for the first time in more than a year. Any questions about whether I could still compete as an elite were answered when I won the national half marathon championship in January 2009. Some people were surprised by my victory in my first race since the summer. I wasn't. Despite all I'd been through in the year-plus since the Olympic Marathon Trials, I never gave up the core belief that I still had untapped potential. Now that I'd rebuilt my body, it was better able to hold up to what I asked of it.

In February, I won the national cross-country championships as a last-minute entry. Here's a peek into the finances of professional running: My Nike contract at the time said that if I finished worse than fourth in a major marathon, my base pay for the year would be reduced significantly. That clause contributed to not running New York in 2008. I had already suffered a reduction clause in 2008 for not making the Olympic team. I couldn't afford another one. My 2009 contract said the top-four marathon clause could be voided by winning the national cross-country title. So I did. That win took pressure off, not only for London—I didn't need to rush things and jeopardize all the progress I'd made over the last several months. I could run London to the best of my current capabilities.

That doesn't mean I was complacent going into London. It would be seventeen months since my last marathon. In that one, I'd finished eighth and failed to make the Olympic team. I had dropped out of the marathon before that. So I really needed a good result. A decent race would be a huge confidence boost and confirmation that my body had emerged from the previous year's trial stronger.

The race itself was one of the more unusual of my career. As with my second marathon, Chicago in 2003, I decided before the start not to go for the win. I wanted to keep the leaders within range, but I also needed to be realistic. Led by the 2008 Olympic champion, Sammy Wanjiru of Kenya, the front pack would be chasing the world record. There were times in my career when I felt capable of running 2:05, but the spring of 2009 wasn't one of them. I had already run 2:09 several times. I wanted to see if I could do that again or even go a little faster. I was part of a second pack that included Dathan Ritzenhein, who had placed ninth and was the top American at the Olympic Marathon. We had a pacer who would take us through halfway at between 2:07 and 2:08 pace. In other words, still plenty fast! (My PR before the race was just under 2:10, and Dathan's was just over 2:11.)

Also as with Chicago, I don't have a lot of distinct memories from those 26.2 miles of running. When I'm racing to win I'm constantly thinking about making moves and covering others' moves. It's an intense experience that creates little snapshots in my mind of key moments. In London, of course I wanted to place as high as possible, but I was more focused on running a good time. My main concern was mile splits that were ambitious but not ridiculous. That's a different approach than something like trying to win the New York City Marathon. There, I might run the stretch on First Avenue faster than 4:40 per mile. You have to if that's what the lead pack does. While you're going that fast, you know the pace will slow again once people have been dropped from the pack.

In contrast, in London there was no reason to throw in a mile or two that fast; when you're mostly racing the clock, doing so will eventually catch up to you and your overall time will be slower. It's an efficient way to run but not the most memorable. I recall that Dathan was eager to pick up the pace at around mile

7 or 8. I said we should let the pacers take us to 17 or 18 miles, and then we could start pushing if we wanted. Early on, we needed to conserve energy. We went through halfway in 1:03:33, right at 2:07 pace, so I felt that holding back earlier was the right decision.

I slowed over the second half while managing stomach cramps and a blister that threw off my form. The race is mostly a blur. Without looking at a picture, I can't remember what jersey I wore. I don't even have a clear mind's-eye view of crossing the line. What was clear was my time—2:09:21, a PR by 32 seconds, a month before my thirty-fourth birthday, when a lot of people had written me off. I was elated, especially after all I'd been through.

PERSONAL RECORDS POINT THE WAY

Afterward Dathan was upset that he'd run 2:10:00. I completely understand why he'd rather have run 2:09:59. Still, I tried to cheer him up. I told him we went out at 2:07 pace and even though we slowed quite a bit in the second half, we both set personal bests. We should be celebrating, not getting down, I told him. It's a message I share with runners wherever I go: Celebrate every personal best, even if it's only by one second.

What does a personal best in running mean? It means you have proof of covering a given distance faster than you ever had in all your time as a runner. That's huge. That's huge in running terms, given how hard we all work and how often obstacles pop up. And that's huge in life terms, and it's part of why racing is so important to so many people. There, in black-and-white terms, is the record of you doing the best you've ever done at this task. It's hard to get that sort of undeniable feedback in a lot of the rest of your life. Were you better at your job last week than ever before?

Better as a spouse, friend, parent? How would you know? Running can give you that undeniable evidence. So celebrate it!

You don't need to race to set personal records. Maybe this month you ran more days than ever before, or you're having your longest injury-free stretch, or you've recently run farther than ever. Celebrate it! Do the same in the rest of your life when you know you've done something better than ever. Take pride in getting that much closer to your best.

Setting a personal record should leave you hungry for more. Just as a great workout isn't a fluke but a hint of your potential, PRs point the way to what else you might achieve. (I wound up setting four more marathon PRs in the five years after London.) After a PR, your set point has been raised. Now figure out how to tap into your potential even more. Even when you PR, there were probably things in training and on race day that could have gone better. Learn from those experiences to make your next PR that much more likely.

I was fired up after London. My body could again go the distance; in fact, it could do so faster than ever. I wasn't injured, and I was back to being able to train well and consistently. At the beginning of the year I'd let New York City race director Mary Wittenberg know I was confident about my future. After London I told Hawi to get my participation in that November's marathon formalized. I felt my time had finally come.

KEY LESSON

Set long-term goals and never let go of those dreams.

I woke up on September 20, 2009, with vivid recall of a dream—I had won the New York City Marathon. I was so excited about the dream that I quickly told Yordanos about it. She was silent for a short while, then asked, "Do you know what happened at the Great North Run today?"

Yordanos told me that at the British half marathon held that morning, Martin Lel of Kenya had run 59:32, which is much faster than I'd run for the distance. Jaouad Gharib of Morocco had run 60:04. I was to face both men in New York in six weeks. I shrugged and said, "Well, I guess I can say good-bye to that dream."

After a short pause, I reconsidered. "I think they peaked too soon," I told Yordanos. "They need to be in peak shape on November first, not today." I got excited again about my dream. I'd been hoping and working to win New York since my debut marathon there in 2002. Through all the challenges over the years—the injuries that limited my training, the logistical debacle of the 2006 race, the near-end of my career after the 2008 Olympic Trials—the idea of winning New York fueled my fire. I truly never stopped believing that I had what it took to meet my goal. By now I'd so internalized that belief that it was playing out in my subconscious.

GET YOURSELF A GOAL

You've probably heard what makes for a good goal. Criteria include:

- It requires you to increase or improve upon what you're currently capable of.
- It can be quantified or otherwise stated so that you know if you reached it.
- It requires intermediate steps so that you know how you're progressing toward it.
- It has a date by which you hope to achieve it.
- It is personally meaningful to you.

These elements of a good goal are all important. For long-term goals, or what you might think of as your dreams, the last criterion is key. If you're going to work for something for many, many months, or years, or maybe even decades, it has to have immense personal meaning to you. You need to feel deep down that reaching that goal is one of the most important things in your life. It has to be something that will motivate you to keep working, to keep having hope, to keep planning and pushing and persevering when things get difficult. Because things will get difficult. The bigger your goal, the longer it will probably take to achieve, and the more likely it is you'll hit obstacles along the way. Only if your goal is something that really speaks to you will you find a way around those obstacles and keep moving, however slowly and meanderingly, toward accomplishing it.

These long-term goals can take many forms. It was the dream of a better future for his family that drove my father to walk 225 miles through dangerous territory and live apart from us for almost five years until we could all leave Eritrea and live in Italy. That dream continued to fuel him as we settled in the United States, and he worked long hours as a janitor or taxi driver to support us. He didn't allow himself to rest until all of his children had an education and a clear path to prosperity. The joy he feels from having reached his goal is still palpable.

One reason that winning New York was so important to me is that I saw it as a fruit of my father's dream. For a child of Eritrea to win the world's largest marathon wearing a USA jersey signified so much. My family and I are proud Americans who cherish our roots. I saw my winning New York as the American dream come true.

There was something special going on in my psyche that fall. I started seeing all sorts of dual meanings to my race in New York. I would run as an American who was born in Eritrea. I would take on the best of the world while also vying for the national championship. I would represent my longtime home of San Diego and Mammoth Lakes, where we had moved permanently that spring. I would win for myself and to honor the memory of Ryan Shay. I prayed in English and Tigrinya, my native language from Eritrea, for these things to come true.

There's magic in visualization. Picturing yourself accomplishing something imprints that image in your brain. The more vivid the image you create—sights, sounds, smells, sensations—

the more real it will seem. Over time, your brain will accept those images as reality, or at least a potential reality. I had long used visualization, but, as I said, something special was happening that fall. When I was running or taking an ice bath or lying in bed before sleep, I'd "see" different scenarios for how the race would play out. I just knew deep down it was going to be a special race. Waking on September 20 and remembering that I'd dreamed about winning shows just how internalized that belief had become.

FROM MIND TO BODY

When I told Yordanos on September 20 about my dream of winning, I did so after going upstairs to our family room. She, too, could feel that something special could happen in New York. Our daughter Fiyori was twenty months old that September. Yordanos was 100 percent behind the idea of me sleeping downstairs so that I wouldn't be woken when she had to get up to tend to Fiyori. That's just one small example of how we've always worked as a team. We runners often get portrayed as solitary figures toiling away on our own. If we're lucky, we have the support of family and friends who help us attain goals that would otherwise be out of our reach.

My training for New York was fantastic. I don't mean that I had interval workouts or tempo runs that were far faster than what I'd done before other marathons. I mean that, week after week after week, I put up solid workouts, long runs, and overall mileage, and I steadily built my fitness. I had no significant injury or health issues. It was great to plan out training and execute it almost like clockwork.

I've always believed that consistency, not isolated killer workouts, is the key to peak performance. Many elite runners could have done any one day, or even any one week, of my training for New York. It's doing those days and weeks over and over again that makes the difference. Your body can gradually get stronger and you can progress your fitness. That's true for runners of all levels. You'll accomplish a lot more by regularly doing 95 percent of your capabilities than by trying to do too much and then losing time to injury, illness, or fatigue.

The only break in training was for the San Jose Rock 'n' Roll Half Marathon four weeks before New York. It wasn't much of a break—I still ran more than 100 miles the week before the race. I went to San Jose hoping to break Ryan Hall's American record of 59:43. Showing again how respect underlies true competition, Ryan told me, "Go get that record" as I left our training base in Mammoth Lakes.

The race organized a pacer to help me break the record. But, similar to what happened with a pacer in my second marathon, I ran most of the race on my own. In San Jose the pacer stopped after 3 miles. I pushed hard by myself for the last 10 miles and won in 1:01:00, which remained my personal record for the rest of my career. Given that I didn't really rest for the race, I felt this was a great result. The time confirmed that I was in great shape, but I could feel that my fitness was still increasing. I hadn't yet peaked.

The week before the marathon, Fiyori got the sniffles. It was the year the swine flu virus was going around. I thought, "Oh my goodness, I'm in the shape of my life and now my daughter is sick." I love my family, but . . . I spent the next couple of days with Brian Ball, a close friend in Mammoth. I also washed my hands more. Doing so was an example of implementing the lesson from New York City in 2006, of minimizing exposure to foreseeable risks.

NEW YORK, NEW YORK

Martin Lel, who had run so fast in that September half marathon, wound up withdrawing soon before the marathon. He had won New York in 2003 and 2007 but this time got injured in his buildup. Lel probably had peaked in September. His withdrawal shows how the most important thing in marathon training is to make it to the start line healthy and with your fitness rising, rather than feeling like you're hanging on. I definitely felt I was in better shape than when I'd won the San Jose half four weeks out.

Good thing, too, that I was so fit. Even with Lel's withdrawal, the field was top-notch. It included James Kwambai of Kenya, who earlier that year became the third-fastest marathoner in history; his compatriot Robert Cheruiyot, a four-time Boston champ who had also won Chicago; and Jaouad Gharib, the reigning Olympic marathon silver medalist. With the U.S. championships occurring within the overall race, the American presence was also strong, including Ryan Hall, my old friend Abdi Abdirahman, and 2008 Olympian Jorge Torres in his marathon debut.

One of the reasons I was so fired up for New York in 2009 was that I'd missed the Olympics in 2008. I saw that fall's marathon as my personal Olympics, an opportunity to prove to myself and others that I could still take on anyone in the world. Wearing a USA jersey in New York added to the feeling that the five boroughs were going to be my own version of the Olympic marathon course.

Right after the race started and I looked around to see all those strong Americans, I said to myself, "Hmm, maybe the U.S. title would be good enough for today." That was just a momentary thought. Once we got going and I was in a good running rhythm, the dream I'd had for so many years reasserted itself. Today could be my day, if I saw and seized opportunities as they arose.

One of the best running tips I ever got came from Yordanos before the race. She told me I was too often being too aggressive too early in the race. Not that I was always pushing the pace from the start. But Yordanos had watched videos of my races and said, "You're doing all the work." She was right: Past halfway, I was often near the front of the pack. I'd been a front-runner since high school. My approach had always been, "We're here for a distance race, not to see who has the best sprint over the last 400 meters. So if you're going to beat me, you're going to need to work hard to do so." Yordanos convinced me that in marathons, that way of running allowed others to draft off me and conserve energy. This time, she told me, tuck in and be a factor later in the race.

My plan was to wait until the last few miles in Central Park to push. The early pace was solid—just over 1:05 at halfway—but nothing outlandish. I told myself to be ready for the usual surges on First Avenue, between miles 16 and 19. I figured the 2004 winner, Hendrick Ramaala of South Africa, would be the one to initiate the fast miles there that had become his trademark. And he did—sort of. The pace picked up and some people were dropped. In the 18th mile I was the sole American among the leaders.

But Hendrick wasn't as bold and quick as he'd been five years earlier. He was trying to get others to help him continue the surges. This told me he wasn't feeling up to breaking the pack on his own, as had been the case in previous years. I stuck with my plan of running as relaxed as possible. The surging wasn't fast or sustained enough to drop those of us, including Cheruiyot and Gharib, hanging back a few seconds and conserving energy.

Yordanos was right: The ones who really paid the price for surging were the front-runners. They had spent energy on the moves without much to show for it. Meanwhile, I still felt strong as a pack of four coalesced after 20 miles: me, Cheruiyot, Kwambai, and Abderrahime Bouramdane of Morocco, who later received a ban from competition for doping. The race was shaping up how I had so often visualized, with the decisive moves being made in Central Park. Cheruiyot and Kwambai occasionally spoke Swahili to each other, so I figured they were discussing tactics. I readied myself for a big move.

It didn't come. Instead, Kwambai and Bouramdane lost contact after a 4:56 22nd mile. It was now just me against Cheruiyot.

MY SHINING HOUR

Cheruiyot had soundly defeated me the last time we raced, at the 2006 Boston Marathon. But I was feeling increasingly confident as we ran by side by side. I was running off his shoulder, still implementing Yordanos's advice. Cheruiyot gestured for me to move alongside him or take the lead. You'll see that often in distance races, where the person leading is bothered by the person drafting. The gesture means, "Share the race. Get up here and do some of the work." I've made that gesture to others, and I've cooperated when others have made it to me.

Not this time, however. I thought, "I hear what you're saying, but I'm not going to do it. Today is the day when I wait and get to the finish line first." I held back. When the person drafting refuses to cooperate, you'll often see the leader take off in a spurt of anger. That's what Eliud Kipchoge did in the 2016 Olympic Marathon when his one remaining challenger ignored Kipchoge's gesture. Kipchoge surged away to win. If you're feeling good and your gesture is refused, then it's common to do what Kipchoge did: "Okay, if you want to draft off me, let's see if you can handle this." When Cheruiyot didn't do something similar, I took that as a sign he was hurting. I stayed tucked in and waited to go into the lead when it was best for me.

We entered Central Park with just more than three miles to run. I was familiar with all the turns and downhills, from my other marathons and shorter races on this stretch. I felt like Cheruiyot was on my home turf. I was planning to make a move in the last mile, at the spot where Ryan Shay passed away in the Olympic Marathon Trials two years earlier. But it happened sooner. I couldn't believe it—on a downhill stretch in the 24th mile, I suddenly had two or three steps on Cheruiyot. This was the moment I'd been dreaming of and working toward for years. It was now up to me to make the most of the opportunity.

I told myself that the next 400 meters were the most crucial stretch of the race. I pushed as hard as I could for the next minute. Finally I was the one using this tactic to win a marathon! I knew that if I got a good gap on Cheruiyot, he'd have a hard time closing it. And I was feeling so strong that, even if he did catch back up, I had more moves up my sleeve.

Later I learned that Cheruiyot started looking back almost immediately, meaning that he had conceded first place and was now focused on protecting second. I kept pushing to build an insurmountable gap. (By the end, I put 53 seconds on Cheruiyot.) I crossed myself when I ran past where Ryan Shay had passed away. "Give me your strength," I prayed. "This is for both of us."

My mind was racing as much as my body: I thought about Ryan, and how proud he would have been of me; I thought, "It's actually happening! I'm going to win my first marathon!" And I thought, "It's not over until the tape touches your chest, so stay focused on good form." I snuck peeks back on the turns to confirm that Cheruiyot wasn't closing, but even then I kept telling myself to keep on task. Doing so was difficult! Joy and amazement overcame me as I reentered Central Park for the final 600 meters. After all I'd been through the previous two years, to have my dream finally become a reality, to hear the crowd cheering "USA! USA!" and my name, to be on the verge of winning my personal Olympics, it was all just overwhelming. I tapped my USA jersey and motioned to the crowd while thinking, "Pinch me, pinch me."

This time, I didn't wake up after dreaming about winning New York. This time, I was living it. Part of me didn't want the race to end. When it did, I was the first American to win New York in twenty-seven years. I had a new personal best of 2:09:15. I was on top of the running world a year after having almost retired. I was living proof that you should never give up on your dreams.

A DREAM REALIZED

I got attention for medaling in the Athens Olympics. But winning New York made me a star. I would be known around the world for the rest of my career by just three letters: Meb.

The aftermath of the race was a whirlwind. I read the Top Ten list on David Letterman's show. I was a guest of honor at a Knicks game, where Chris Paul asked how I had the energy to do a push-up at the end of a marathon. I got VIP treatment atop the Empire State Building. Later that month I rode a float with Miss America and a Statue of Liberty replica in the Macy's Thanksgiving Day Parade. Winning New York was also a nice boost to my bank account, especially after the struggles of the preceding two years.

The public recognition was a great payoff for having met my goal of winning New York. But the real reward was internal. I've always wanted my kids to know what their dad did. There's a picture from after New York of me with Yordanos, our girls, Hawi, our parents, and Coach Larsen. To be able to show that to my daughters once they were old enough to understand was priceless. I still draw strength and motivation from memories of that day.

I've said how winning New York was a dream of mine for years. How do you maintain hope that your long-term goals can come true? How do you keep working toward them even when it seems like they're getting more out of reach, not closer? I can tell you from my experience that the key is what I talked about at the beginning of this chapter—setting the right goals. You'll know when you've hit on the right ones. They're the ones that will still call to you no matter how challenging things get. They're the ones that make your life better just by chasing them.

After winning New York, I had one more of those lifetime running goals: to win the Boston Marathon. I took my next shot at it the following spring.

KEY LESSON

It's better to be 90 percent ready and make it to the start line than to panic and become either overtrained or unable to start the race.

S poiler alert: I didn't follow up my win in New York City with the Boston Marathon title. Well, at least not immediately. I was hampered by a knee problem during my buildup for the 2010 edition of Boston. Although the knee was fine by race day, I lost too much training time to be able to vie for the win.

After I finished fifth at Boston that year, some people said my New York win was a fluke. Others said I'd lost focus. Still others seemed surprised that I wasn't upset about my result. None of that was the case. Sure, I wanted to win Boston. (Who doesn't?) But afterward I had renewed faith that breaking the tape on Boylston Street was still a very real possibility for me.

FOCUS, FOCUS, FOCUS

The runner's version of "Dance with the one who brought you" is "Stick to the routine that has brought you success." In running as in other fields, you'll see people accomplish something huge and then never again approach that level of achievement. In some cases, it's because the trappings of success distract them. This phenomenon is common among runners from Kenya and Ethiopia who quickly go from living on next to nothing to winning what in their countries is a fortune. They then lose the discipline that contributed to their accomplishments.

In other cases, people stay just as committed but they change their approach. A musician or author wishing not to repeat herself might try an entirely new creative method. Athletes can also feel like they need to shake things up—they'll start working with a new coach or revamp their training program on the theory that the body needs a new stimulus to move past its current capabilities.

That was never my thinking. I worked with Coach Larsen from college straight on through the end of my professional career. I relied on the same staples (long runs, tempo runs, and interval workouts) during my fifteen years as a competitive marathoner. As I noted earlier, a hallmark of my career was consistency. For several years I was among the handful of guys in any marathon with a real shot at winning. At my level, who won on a given day depended in part on who was the healthiest during his buildup, who had the right mind-set on race day, and who best realized and capitalized on opportunities during the race.

So after winning New York, I wasn't tempted to shake things up. I will admit that the post-victory hoopla and broadening fame were new elements. Much of that occurred, however, while I was taking my usual break from real training in the weeks after the marathon. I knew it was important not to get off track. Loving the process of training, and simply loving running, always made it easy for me to put my head down and get back to work when the time came.

As always, a key part of that routine was training at altitude. Training at altitude has many advantages: increased red blood cell production, which improves your aerobic capacity; regular testing of your tenacity, as you live and run in thin air; and few distractions, because you're usually secluded in a quiet location. Training at altitude also has its challenges.

WATCHING MY FITNESS SLIP AWAY

In the United States, training at altitude in the winter is going to mean snow. Mammoth Lakes is well situated in that you can get to significantly lower altitude, where there's less snow, in about forty minutes. I considered that my commute. Even in good weather, I usually made that drive for key workouts. The Round Valley area of Bishop sits at about 4,100 feet. That's high enough to still give some of the benefits but low enough to allow for faster workouts.

Most of the time, however, you're living amid snow. Doing so was my undoing before Boston that year. One day in late January I was clearing snow off the car. There was ice underneath the snow in the driveway, and I slipped on it and landed hard on my left knee. A week later, I fell on the knee again, this time while leaving the gym at seven thirty p.m. and learning the hard way that the snow that had melted during daylight had refrozen. The knee hurt when I ran. Trying to train through the discomfort only aggravated it. Pretty soon I was dealing with the early stages of patellar tendinitis. Such injuries are among the most frustrating, because they're not initially caused by training mistakes or being lax about strength training or something else you can analyze and take steps to avoid in the future. They just happen during everyday life, and your running winds up suffering mightily.

The 100-plus-mile weeks I'd been hitting quickly became a memory. I missed a lot of days of training. Some of the days when I did run were short, easy runs on the treadmill. (I wanted both reliable footing and the option to end a run as soon as possible if the knee started bothering me.) Despite my babying the knee, it wouldn't improve. January ended with me not running its last four days. After starting February with another day off, I ran 35 minutes on the treadmill on February 2, then 40 minutes on February 3, and then . . . I took another day off.

By this point I'd been feeling increasingly sorry for myself. After that early-February day off, I wrote in my log, "Get your head in the game." Boston was only two and a half months away. I needed to be doing something every day, even if it was as little as 20 minutes of treadmill running followed by 20 minutes of swimming.

This improved mind-set helped when things got even worse physically. I started the second week of February with a 7.5-mile run, my longest in a while. And I ended the week with a total of 7.5 miles—my knee still balked whenever I tried to get back toward the type of training I needed to be doing for Boston. I told myself that Boston might be out of the question, but I didn't need to decide immediately. I'd been in this situation before. From that experience I knew the right approach was to be patient.

RUNNING, BUT RUNNING OUT OF TIME

That patience was rewarded. I resumed running the second week of February and got in 38 miles that week, followed by 68 miles the following week. Obviously my situation was still far from ideal. But I'm guessing you know the wonderful feeling of seeing progress after weeks of setbacks. It's always such a relief to feel like you've weathered a test.

By late February my mind and body were finally back on the same page. I don't know how, but when I resumed adding quality to my mileage I had great workouts immediately. One of my first hard efforts was an 8-mile tempo run in 38:47 (a little slower than 4:50 per mile). I was able to build on that with a 10-mile tempo run at almost the same pace, and then a 15-mile tempo run at just under 5:00 per mile. To put that tempo run in perspective, that's the first 15 miles of a 2:10 marathon, at a moderately high altitude of 4,000 feet.

These tempo runs occurred within the larger context of increased weekly mileage (I peaked at 111 miles during that buildup) and good long runs (I was able to work up to a 23-miler and a 25-miler). By early April, when it was time to start tapering for the marathon, I had come a long way since the desperate days of two months earlier. The training I was able to put together gave me hope that although I probably wouldn't be able to win Boston, I could still go there and really compete.

I'm going into all this detail to give as clear a picture as possible about what was going on with my body and in my mind. I lost a lot of time waiting for the knee to come around. I was able to get going again at good volume with good quality, but I ran out of time to be ready to win the world's most prestigious marathon.

What to do in these situations is always going to be a judgment call. One thing you definitely shouldn't do is force the issue: Don't push too hard or rush things in an attempt to make up for lost time. Even my 100-plus-mile weeks after not running a month earlier were cautious, logical progressions from what I'd been doing. I increased my mileage as doing so felt good and didn't cause the knee problem to return or new ones to arise. I used the same process for increasing the length of my tempo runs and long runs. I probably could have immediately gone back to a 15-mile tempo run or a 25-mile long run. But the extra benefit wouldn't have been worth it for the increased risk. It's always better to be undertrained than overtrained. That's especially the case when you're returning from time off and have the running version of a deadline looming on your calendar. Showing up on the start line at 90 percent fitness is far preferable to not being on the start line because you rushed things and got hurt or sick.

As a professional athlete, I faced these situations perhaps more often. When I was hurt before the 2004 Olympic Marathon Trials, regrouping for another marathon a couple months later wasn't an option—the road to the Athens Olympics went only through the Trials course in Birmingham, Alabama. You might have more flexibility in your schedule and opt for a backup race. That's definitely the way to go if running your original race is going to be really frustrating or if you're still hurt the week of the race.

A lot of times, though, sticking with your original race and adjusting your goals for it is probably the right choice. Marathons and the expenses related to them aren't cheap. Your and your family's routine may have been altered for months as you trained. In life in general, it's rare that things go perfectly, or even how we'd like them to. There's something to be said for being the sort of person who adapts to and absorbs adversity, shows up as planned, and does the best that's possible on the day.

BACK TO BOSTON

That was certainly my mind-set standing on the start line in Hopkinton. I was pretty sure a win wasn't in the cards. But a good result was still possible, and it was important that I do everything I could to make that happen. Early on, the lead pack and my body were amazingly cooperative in helping me toward that good result. The overall pace was within my capabilities, nobody was throwing in crazy surges, and my legs felt fine. I was still with the leaders as we passed the 17-mile mark and made the famous right-hand turn at the Newton Fire Station.

Just after we made that turn I felt something in my left quad. I told myself the Newton hills, including Heartbreak Hill, were coming up, and that the leaders probably wouldn't be hammering up them. "If I can keep in contact with them," I thought, "then maybe by the time we're through the hills my leg will feel better and I can chase people down over the final miles."

My leg had other ideas. The pain in my quad kept increasing, and I couldn't take advantage of the fast stretch of miles after cresting Heartbreak Hill. My mind was telling my body that now was the time to start rolling, but my body couldn't execute. The leaders got more and more out of sight. I didn't fall apart horribly or anything like that. I just couldn't go faster when that was the thing to do. Miles 20 through 24 were all in the range of 5:05 to 5:10 per mile. Over the last two miles I slowed to a little over 5:20 per mile. The pace felt comfortable aerobically, but my quad more or less gave up on me.

I finished fifth in 2:09:26. I dug deeper those last few miles in Boston than I did when winning New York. Many people think that when you win it's because you worked harder than ever. The truth is that when you're "on," races often feel easier.

Up ahead, Robert Kiprono Cheruiyot of Kenya was "on" and won in 2:05:52 to shatter the previous course record of 2:07:13, set by Robert Kipkoech Cheruiyot in 2006. (Kipkoech Cheruiyot is the runner who won Boston four times and who I'd beaten in New York the previous fall.)

I later learned I had ruptured my quad muscle. Obviously,

I wish that hadn't happened. Still, that year's Boston was a key race in my career. It strengthened my belief that I could win Boston. Despite the ruptured quad, I had run 30 seconds faster on the Boston course than I had four years earlier, and only 11 seconds off the personal best I'd set in New York. Those last two miles in the 5:20s alone put an extra 40 seconds on what my time might otherwise have been. And I'd run that fast just two months after resuming training. All of that told me that I could run under 2:09 on the Boston course. Most years, that will get you the victory there. I just needed to get to the start line healthy.

#1, New York City, 2002: Just a few strides into my first marathon (I'm in the black hat, toward the left). A little more than two hours later, I swore it would also be my last. Little did I know . . .

#2, Chicago, 2003: Mission accomplished! My second marathon was a rare case of racing the clock, not my competitors. I easily attained the Olympic qualifying time.

#3, Olympic Trials, 2004: Coach Bob Larsen and I worked together for more than two decades. We shared many special moments, some in private, some in public, such as making my second Olympic team.

#4, Athens Olympics, 2004:
It was a great honor to be the first American man to win an Olympic marathon medal in twenty-eight years.

#5, New York City, 2004:
I'm not one who rests on his laurels. Just ten weeks after winning an Olympic medal, I returned to New York, fought for the win, and placed second.

#6, New York City, 2005:
Trying my hardest to stay with world record holder Paul Tergat *(far left)* and the defending champ, Hendrick Ramaala. Finishing third on limited training told me I could win New York one day.

#7, Boston, 2006: The marathon is all about patience. I relearned that lesson the hard way by being too aggressive too soon in my first race on the Boston course.

#8, New York City, 2006: Weakened by food poisoning, I was unable to stay with my fellow U.S. Olympian Dathan Ritzenhein in his debut marathon. This was my first really subpar marathon.

#9, London, 2007: The only marathon in my career I didn't finish was my first one at London. Khalid Khannouchi, to my immediate left, also dropped out, and that helped me accept that I'd made the right decision.

#10, Olympic Trials, 2007: This was probably the hardest race of my life. Rather than battling eventual winner Ryan Hall for the victory, I finished eighth, physically and emotionally broken.

#11, London, 2009: Setting a personal best in my first marathon in almost a year and a half was a huge step in my comeback from significant injury.

#12, New York City, 2009: Never give up hope. Living my dream of winning New York was that much sweeter after being injured for most of the previous year.

#13, Boston, 2010: I ruptured my quad during this race but still ran faster than I had my first time on the Boston course. This gave me confidence I could win Boston if I stayed healthy and focused.

#14, New York City, 2010: All smiles despite not being able to defend my title. I consider races that fall short of goals to be learning experiences, not disappointments.

#16, Olympic Trials, 2012: The marathon rewards those who ration their resources. I waited until late in the race and then made one big move to get away from Ryan Hall for the win.

#15, New York City, 2011: Fired up finishing my first race with my new shoe sponsor, Skechers! Setting a personal best despite a foot wound and vomiting showed me I could still compete with the best.

#17, London Olympics, 2012: Fighting my way from twenty-first to fourth at the Olympics inspired me to keep competing and dreaming of a Boston win.

#18, New York City, 2013: My slowest marathon was one of my most gratifying. This finish with Mike Cassidy resonated with runners and others who know the biggest accomplishment is often to just keep going.

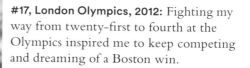

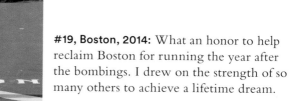

#19, Boston, 2014: What an honor to help reclaim Boston for running the year after the bombings. I drew on the strength of so many others to achieve a lifetime dream.

#20, New York City, 2014:
There's great mutual respect among marathoners because we know how hard each other works. Here I am with fellow New York champions Wilson Kipsang *(center)* and Geoffrey Mutai.

#21, Boston, 2015:
None of us really runs alone. Unable to defend my Boston title, I wanted to finish with a fellow marathoner and sped up to cross the line with local Hilary Dionne.

#22, New York City, 2015:
Celebrating an American masters record at age 40. There are always new worthwhile goals to pursue in running and life.

#23, Olympic Trials, 2016:
Making my fourth Olympic team at age 41. The accomplishment was especially sweet because so many family and friends were there in the city where I went to college.

#24, Rio Olympics, 2016:
Still running to win at age 42 in my final Olympics, sixteen years after my first Games.

#25, Boston, 2017:
My final Boston was one of the toughest marathons of my career. The crowds helped me reach the finish with my head held high.

#26, New York City, 2017:
Tired, but proud to have given it my all, both in my final competitive marathon and throughout my career.

Although I'm retired from elite competition, I'm still at a lot of races. I love sharing the joy and rewards of running with others.

KEY LESSON

It's important to enjoy the fruits of your labor, but it's more important to set new goals and focus on the future.

Throughout my career, more often than not I wasn't able to win a major race two years in a row. There's a simple reason for that: These days, almost nobody regularly repeats as the champion of a major race. The level of competition in professional distance running is simply too high. What's noteworthy is when someone does win back-to-back titles, not when they don't. At New York, the last man to win two years in a row was John Kagwe of Kenya, the 1997 and 1998 champion. (Kagwe's countryman Geoffrey Mutai won two *editions* in a row, 2011 and 2013, after Hurricane Sandy forced the cancellation of the 2012 race.)

I'm not saying this to make excuses for finishing sixth, not first, the year after my New York City Marathon victory.

I certainly prepared with every intention of winning again, and on the start line I thought the title was mine to protect. It just turned out not to be my day.

Was my so-so result the consequence of enjoying my 2009 win just a little too much? I don't think so. As I've mentioned, I like to accomplish one goal and then move on to the next challenge. If anything, I've sometimes had to work at better enjoying the rewards of my accomplishments.

Striking the balance between celebrating in the present and focusing on the future can be tough for many runners. A lot of us are driven, results-oriented people in most parts of our lives. We often have that gnawing what-now feeling after hitting a big goal. We sometimes feel guilty or worried about relaxing our usual standards. We have to be disciplined about temporarily dropping our usual discipline.

Fortunately, the marathon has a built-in way to encourage those short-term celebrations. The smart choice in the few weeks afterward is to not run much and to regroup physically and mentally for your next running goal. That's the perfect time to live it up a little—stay up late, sleep in, have two desserts, be lazy, congratulate yourself rather than push yourself. Enjoying your success isn't being complacent. It's a key part of the transition to getting fired up for what's next.

ONLY CONNECT

Also, enjoying the fruits of your labor isn't synonymous with not working hard. My greatest reward from winning New York wasn't the money, fame, TV appearances, or honors like being in the Macy's Thanksgiving Day Parade. It was the opportunity to connect with so many more of my fellow runners.

Born in 1975, I was sort of the last of the old guard in terms of information environments. In high school and college, I followed running via newspapers and magazines. That was it for connecting with others and knowing what was going on. The Internet changed how I got my running news, but things really took off around the time I won the New York City Marathon in 2009. Suddenly everyone was on social media. With that phenomenon coinciding with my becoming more known in the culture at large, suddenly I had a way to reach people and inspire them in a way that wasn't possible when I medaled in the 2004 Olympics.

I got on Twitter in the fall of 2009. I remember seeing that I had five hundred followers and thinking, "Who are these five hundred people?" Then it was one thousand, then two thousand, and I thought, "Wait, what is this?" I love connecting with fellow runners and hearing their stories. Early on, I felt like I needed to reply to everyone who wrote to me on social media. My upbringing emphasized the importance of being polite and respectful. Eventually I realized I couldn't apply those principles as I had been doing and respond to everyone. I could, however, try to send messages that a lot of people would find meaning in.

My in-person connections with other runners also dramatically increased after I won New York. That victory led to many more expo appearances and other meet-and-greet occasions. Winning New York also resulted in a *Runner's World* feature and other articles that detailed my story of recovery and renewal, of going from the nadir of the 2008 Olympic Marathon Trials to attaining a lifetime dream in 2009. People connected with my story of recovery and renewal. It wasn't just winning New York—it was doing so after an injury that almost ended my career. People would tell me that my story gave them resolve to overcome their own challenges. Some had to do with running, but many were about other parts of life. I'd hear from people in their sixties and seventies that I'd inspired them, and I'd think, "Wow, how do I respond to that?" Hearing their stories really drove home a new responsibility that I had to be a positive role model. Running was simply the means through which I could encourage people to work a little harder, dream a little bigger, persevere a bit longer.

BACK TO THE FIVE BOROUGHS

Heading into New York, I had every reason to believe I could repeat as champion. My training was as solid as ever, with several consecutive weeks between 105 and 120 miles. I did some of my longest long runs ever—a 26-miler, a 27-miler, and a 28.5-miler, at high altitude. I returned to the San Jose Half Marathon, which I'd won four weeks before winning New York, and repeated as champion in a fast time, three minutes ahead of second place.

Of course, winning New York is always a tall order. The marquee name for that year's race was Haile Gebrselassie of Ethiopia, a two-time Olympic champion and four-time world champion on the track who set more than two dozen world records in his career. It's an understatement to say Haile had made a successful transition to the roads. Two years earlier, he won the Berlin Marathon in 2:03:59, becoming the first person to break 2:04 for the distance. That was still the world record as we lined up on Staten Island.

Not that Haile was invincible. He was thirty-seven years old and starting to feel the effects of so many years of hard training and racing. He occasionally dropped out of shorter races with various physical problems. The night before New York, we started hearing he might not start because of knee tendinitis.

Still, Haile had run a very fast half marathon a month and a half earlier and had won his previous six marathons. He would set the tone of the first part of the race.

A large group of us passed halfway in 1:05:19, a typical first-half time in New York. Most of the guys in the pack were still keying off Haile. It was going to be interesting to see if there would be the usual moves on First Avenue, in miles 17–19. Sometimes a key person like that means that others defer to his presence. They might think, "This is perhaps the greatest distance runner ever. Will I really break him with just a few fast miles at that point in the race? I might just waste energy and then be unable to go when he starts racing later. I better sit tight." With someone the stature of Haile, that can happen even when you know he started the race a little vulnerable.

Make that very vulnerable. Haile stopped running as we exited the 59th Street Bridge a little after the 16-mile mark. His knee pain was too great. His withdrawal immediately changed the tenor of the race. He told his countryman Gebre Gebremariam, who was making his marathon debut, to move to the front and start pushing. Gebremariam, in turn, told me to go with him. We were familiar with each other from the European track circuit. He had a long and impressive career on the track and was the 2009 world cross-country champion. He also spoke Tigrinya, an Eritrean language. I had even given him advice on how to race the New York course, telling him that if he had a choice, don't really start racing until he sees the green of Central Park.

I was unable to surge with Gebremariam. It was frustrating. My interval workouts and tempo runs in my buildup had been good. There was no reason I shouldn't have been able to quickly shift pace. But I couldn't. My legs just wouldn't go. My brain was doing all the right things. "Cover the move, defend your title, quick feet, you've trained for this, prove that 2009 wasn't a fluke," I told myself. For whatever reason, my body couldn't execute. I couldn't cover the first big move of the race. I wasn't going to repeat as champion. (Gebremariam won in 2:08:14. At least I could take solace in learning he'd followed my advice by waiting until the 25th mile to push hard for the victory.)

Once I lost contact, it wasn't like I slowed dramatically. I didn't have any significantly slower miles or bodily issues that affected my form. I was just sort of there physically. In terms of position in the field, I was mostly running by myself, very occasionally picking off a straggler from the lead pack. I was still digging deep, hoping to rally, hoping enough guys would be hurting that I could wind up on the podium. I kept up my usual self-talk about pace, form, and tiered goals.

Unfortunately, I also had another internal monologue going on, one that hurt rather than helped my performance. If you're like me, you're often asked what you think about when you run. I'm not going to lie—in those final miles of New York, my financial future was weighing heavily on my mind.

I mentioned an odd clause in my Nike contract in Chapter 11. It said that my base pay for the year would be reduced if I didn't finish in one of the top four spots in a major marathon. That clause was still in my contract as I ran in no-man's-land over the last 10 miles of New York in 2010. I had finished fifth in Boston in April. Unless I worked my way past several more runners, I was going to again place out of the top four, and get hammered financially. A disadvantage of being a marathoner is that you have only two shots a year to meet those obligations, unlike athletes in other events who can compete more frequently.

There was the immediate consequence of my base pay being significantly reduced. There was also the longer-term matter of my contract with Nike being up for renewal at the end of 2010.

I hadn't factored in Boston earlier that year. Now I was failing to repeat as New York champion, or even to come close to battling for the win. I was thirty-five years old, an age usually considered past a marathoner's prime. How much of this would be held against me when it came to negotiate for 2011 and beyond? Hawi had received verbal interest from Nike that they wanted to renew my contract, but we had nothing in writing, and Nike had a reputation for not being loyal to its athletes. These are not great thoughts to have coursing through your mind when you're competing against some of the best marathoners in the world.

We all have tough days, in training, racing, and life in general. Even on your best days you probably have to weather tough patches. With experience, you learn how to refute or ignore the negative thoughts that plague you in those moments. You learn how to refocus and break the downward spiral of negative thoughts leading to worse performance, which leads to more negative thoughts, which lead to even worse performance, and so on. I usually break free with both physical and psychological messages to myself. Physically, I concentrate on specific elements of my running form—are my shoulders relaxed, is my cadence light and quick—to reset my attention to the task at hand. Psychologically, I think about why I'm doing what I'm doing, reminding myself that these negative thoughts are inevitable but they don't have to win.

I tried every trick in my bag that day in New York. Seeing other runners ahead to chase down was a big help. Still, it was a long day mentally at the office. Being so far out of contention for the win, I felt like I wasn't meeting expectations—mine or the race organizers' or my sponsors'. Also, by this point Yordanos and I had three daughters. I thought about my responsibility to them. I worried about our financial future. A separate business venture I'd invested in had failed, and I'd lost a lot of cash. I felt like I was letting them and all of my new fans and, yes, myself down.

I crossed the line sixth in 2:11:38, more than two minutes slower than I'd run to win the year before. There was none of the elation of 2009, and little of the usual post-marathon pride. I still strongly believed I could achieve more great things in running. But the path to getting there was looking less certain.

2011 NEW YORK CITY MARATHON

NOVEMBER 6, 2011

PLACE **6th**   TIME   **2:09:13**

KEY LESSON

Always pay attention to detail, but don't let small mistakes keep you from doing what you're capable of.

I n the 2nd mile of the 2011 New York City Marathon, I felt something odd on my left foot. The rest of the lead pack and I were on the downhill portion of the Verrazano-Narrows Bridge. Every time I pushed off with my left foot I had a prickling sensation on the pad under the ball of my foot. It wasn't that something was wrong with my foot; it was that something was *against* my foot.

What's going on, I wondered. Had a pebble or some gritty piece of road debris worked its way into my shoe in just a few minutes of running? Then a thought came to me. I brought a hand to my nose. I should have felt a Breathe Right strip. I didn't. I realized that the strip I'd transported to the start in my left shoe was still in there.

I had two options: Stop, take off my shoe, remove the strip, put my shoe back on, and try to catch up to some of the world's fastest marathoners. Or race 26.2 miles with a Breathe Right strip trapped under my left big toe.

It was more important than usual that I do well in New York in 2011. The race was my only marathon of the year, and my first with a new shoe sponsor, Skechers. To this day, I'm unsure whether I made the right call in dealing with the strip. But I am sure that those two-plus hours started a blessed second phase of my marathon career that surprised even me.

END OF AN ERA

On New Year's Day 2011, Yordanos, the girls, and I packed for a winter of altitude training in Mammoth Lakes. Instead of taking the end of the year to regroup and relax, I felt I had to prove myself anew, as if I were a rookie runner instead of the only American with an Olympic Marathon medal and a New York City title. I considered a great performance in a spring marathon an absolute necessity.

The worry about my Nike contract that gnawed at me in the 2010 New York City Marathon turned out to be well founded. Despite being a highly successful Nike athlete for twelve years, I was offered less than half of what I'd been making. Hawi and I argued our case and asked for a reasonable level of support for just the next two years. The 2012 Olympic Marathon Trials would be held the following January, a little more than twelve months away. I was confident I could make that team. My plan at the time was to retire after the 2013 New York City Marathon. I was looking forward to finishing my career with my longtime sponsor; wearing its logo was widely viewed as a sign that you'd made it to the big time. I wanted to end my career with that aura . . . but I needed to support my family. I told Hawi to tell Nike "no" for the amount offered and with the reduction clauses. Before Hawi could negotiate or give his feedback, Nike withdrew the offer. Their withdrawal made my decision easy in the moment, but I knew that a long professional struggle was ahead.

Then came more bad news. Hawi and I had been talking for months with the person in charge of recruiting the elite field for the Boston Marathon. "We'll let you know in August," we were told. Then it was October. Then November, and then December. In January, once I was no longer with Nike, we finally heard from Boston. Like Nike's, their offer was considerably below market rate. Hawi and I agreed we couldn't accept it. I wondered if I would ever run Boston again. I wrote a post on my website explaining my side of the story, which got a tremendous response from fans.

Bad things come to mind when you're running alone in the snow in January and your professional future is suddenly uncertain. It didn't help that soon afterward I got injured. This was one of the lowest points in my career. Yet I didn't lose hope. After the 2008 Olympic Trials and the trying times that followed, I was able to persevere because I believed I hadn't tapped out my God-given talent. That belief was borne out when I set PRs in both marathons I ran in 2009 and won New York. Struggling through the snow in 2011, with no idea how things were going to work out, I still had that belief. I still felt I could do more—more PRs, another Olympic berth, and the real glimmering prize in my mind's eye, a Boston Marathon title.

Hawi and I eventually found others who shared that belief. In August 2011, I signed with Skechers. I was their first ambassador as they entered the running market. They were serious about making great running shoes. I was serious about doing more great things in running shoes.

DECISION TIME, WAY TOO EARLY

Wanting to represent Skechers well—and to justify their faith in me—added an extra layer of motivation to New York. Even though Skechers signed me to gain credibility via my name, I had promised them I could PR in the half marathon and marathon, and that I could contend for titles in Boston and New York. Even if I didn't win, I felt like I was holding up my end of the partnership if I finished as the top American. Those considerations were among the swirl of thoughts I had once I realized the Breathe Right strip was trapped under my left big toe: How would it look if a shoe mishap ruined my race, even though the shoe had nothing to do with the problem? The takeaway for a lot of people would be "Meb Bombs in First Race in Skechers."

But wait, you're wondering: Why did I have a Breathe Right strip in my shoe in the first place?

You may have noticed by now I like routine. On race day, having a go-to routine saves mental energy—you know what to bring and where to put it, you don't have to think about how far to warm up or what stretches to do, and so on. For years, I put my phone in the right pocket and a Breathe Right strip and ChapStick in the left pocket of the warm-up pants I wore to the start. Like I said, however, Skechers was new to running. They hadn't yet fully rolled out their line, and the pants I wore that day didn't have pockets. Neither did the jacket. So when I packed for the start the night before, I stashed the Breathe Right strip in my left racing shoe, along with the ChapStick.

Another part of my pre-race routine is the switch from training shoes, which I wear for my warm-up run, to racing shoes. When I first put the racing flats on, I single-knot them. Then I do 100-meter strides at race pace or faster. It's almost always the case that, while doing strides, I'll find I need to readjust my socks, or my shoes are tied too tightly, or something like that. I make whatever adjustment is needed, and then double-knot my shoes. That day in New York, everything felt fine on my strides. With no adjustments needed, I double-knotted my racing flats and unknowingly trapped the Breathe Right strip. I did a live TV interview just before the start, and then we were off.

The strip announced its presence in the 2nd mile. I thought stopping to remove the strip would mean taking off my shoe and the knee-length compression sock I had on. If you're familiar with compression gear, you know that its effectiveness depends on its close fit. Getting the shoe and sock off and back on could easily take a minute, if not longer. I would then be a quarter mile or so behind the leaders and spend a lot of energy rejoining the pack. Of course, I later realized I wouldn't have had to remove the sock—the strip was inside my shoe. But in that moment of panic, I wasn't able to think clearly. I decided to keep running and deal with the consequences.

HEAD DOWN, CHIN UP

The sensation under the ball of my left foot gradually went from prickling to stinging to painful. By the 10-mile mark I started to feel the damage of the sharp, hard plastic that you unpeel to apply a Breathe Right strip. It's pretty much impossible not to notice such a thing abrading your foot 90 to 100 times a minute, which is how often my left foot was pushing off on top of the strip.

But there was no stopping now. The field was headed by Kenya's Geoffrey Mutai. He had won Boston in April in an eye-popping 2:03:02, at the time the fastest marathon ever run. (His time didn't count as an official world record because of Boston's point-to-point course and net elevation drop, but still, that's *fast*!) Emmanuel Mutai (unrelated to Geoffrey) was also there. Emmanuel had a reputation for pushing the pace early on. Geoffrey liked to push hard over the second half. Defending champ Gebre Gebremariam was more of a last-mile kicker. Tsegaye Kebede of Ethiopia, the 2008 Olympic bronze medalist, liked to run even pace and chase people down over the last 10K.

With everyone trying to neutralize the others' strengths, the pace was quick from the start. We passed through halfway in 1:03:18, well under what was course-record pace at the start of the race. Setting aside the issue with my foot, I was fine with that pace. This was one of the marathons I entered feeling capable of running 2:07 on a good day on the New York course, which is much more difficult than a flat marathon.

The only good thing about the issue with my foot was that I couldn't see the damage being done. I could certainly feel it, and with every step. The strip was rubbing against the area that had become so raw and traumatized in 2007 and that had bothered me ever since. After every marathon, that part of my foot was like a war wound that was newly aggravated. It was hard not to think about how much worse it would be this time.

That was especially the case because I entered the race knowing that I'd be running another marathon, the 2012 Olympic Trials, just sixty-nine days later. At a pre-race press conference I was asked if the Trials would affect my strategy in New York. If things weren't going well, would I ease in to the finish, or maybe drop out, so that I'd be fresher for the Trials? I tried to put that question out of my mind before the race, but now it resurfaced. There comes a point—or sometimes several points—in every marathon where you think, "Why am I doing this?! Stop!" We all learn how to override those urges. Doing so was more difficult than usual this time because of my worsening foot wound. I was thinking it about every step, and altering my form to land more on the outside of my foot. Resolving to finish despite the foot issue was truly a case of mind over matter.

DAMAGED, BUT NOT DEFEATED

I was still in the lead pack past the 20-mile mark. The pace remained hot. I was thinking that, even with the problem inside my left shoe, this was going to be the day for a huge personal best.

Then, suddenly, those thoughts were interrupted. I felt like someone had hit me in the stomach. I started vomiting. I staggered, slowed, and vomited some more. The leaders sped away from me. Jaouod Gharib of Morocco, the 2008 Olympic silver medalist, had earlier lost contact with the pack. He passed me while I was stopped. The idea of dropping out flitted across my mind again. I told myself two things: No, today I will finish no matter what. So get Gharib so that you're not alone in no-man's-land the last five miles.

Almost immediately after I caught Gharib, it was like I was hit again. I stopped and staggered and vomited. I resumed running. Two hundred meters later, it happened again. And so it continued to the finish—get a good pace going again, suffer another bout of vomiting, regain momentum, ignore my foot, another stop to vomit, pick up speed, dig deeper and deeper until, finally, I was in the last few hundred meters running as hard as I could to that finish line.

As I finished I looked at the clock and saw that, despite all that had happened during the race, I'd set a personal record. My time of 2:09:13 was two seconds faster than I'd run to win two years earlier. On a day when the race record books were rewritten, that performance got me sixth rather than first place. Geoffrey Mutai won in 2:05:05, more than two and a half minutes under the old course record of 2:07:44. Emmanuel Mutai and Tsegaye Kebede also broke the previous course mark. Gebre Gebremariam ran 2:07:59, 15 seconds faster than his winning time the year before, but this time he was fourth. The race remains the fastest and deepest men's contest in New York City Marathon history. I was proud to have been part of it.

In the process I earned the respect of the fastest marathoner in the world. After the race Geoffrey Mutai told me, "You are fit and a tough runner; I was watching you during the race. What's next?" I said the Olympic Trials in sixty-nine days. He said, "Easy." There's a good example of the different mental outlook of African and American runners. Most Americans didn't run Chicago or New York that fall because they thought they wouldn't have enough recovery time before the Trials. After the Trials, I saw Geoffrey at the NYC Half Marathon. He told Mary Wittenberg, then the president and CEO of the New York Road Runners, "Meb is my hero." I thought, "Wow—the guy who set course records at Boston and New York in the same year is calling me his hero."

I drew on my 2011 New York experience for the rest of my career. If something bad happened during a race, like missing my bottle at an aid station, I was able to tell myself it's not a big deal. "Remember, you PRed while vomiting and getting a foot wound; you can get past this little glitch," I would think. Having overcome such obstacles made it easier to put smaller issues in perspective.

I remained dedicated to detail and planning. The lesson from my 2006 New York experience—minimize exposure to predictable risks—was always with me. As I said earlier, a tried-

and-true pre-race routine helped my performance by sparing me from devoting mental energy to lots of small decisions.

But New York 2011 really drove home that if things don't go how I want, they usually will still turn out okay. Absorbing that lesson makes it easier to keep giving your best on challenging days.

KEY LESSON

When you're fit, you don't have to start from scratch. Don't panic if you encounter obstacles en route to your next goal.

A silver lining of being shut out of the 2011 Boston Marathon was that I could run that year's New York City race and still compete well in the 2012 Olympic Marathon Trials. The Trials race, where the three-person team for the London Olympics in August would select itself, was held in mid-January in Houston. Three marathons in nine months would have been risky, because the most important of the three would be run last. By not doing Boston, I was fresh coming into New York. Then all I had to do was recover from that race, get in a short block of training for the Trials, and try to make my third Olympic team.

That plan sounded great on paper. I would have sixty-nine days between marathons, one day fewer than the turnaround I had in my successful Athens Olympics–New York City double in 2004. Of course, I'd be eight years older. But I'd also be eight years wiser. In 2004, my youth was the key to doing well in both marathons—I could hammer hard, recover quickly, and get away with seeing just how much my body could take. Now, at age thirty-six, my experience would be key. I would be guided by my longtime adage that training is 90 percent physical/10 percent mental, while racing is 90 percent mental/10 percent physical.

Well, you know what they say about the best-laid plans. When I mapped out the NYC/Trials double, my plan didn't include being unable to run for almost half of the time between the two races.

NOT THE RECOVERY I ENVISIONED

As I've said, after losing several layers of skin under the base of the big toe on my left foot in 2007, that area was a mess after every marathon. It became much more than a mess after the Breathe Right incident at New York in 2011. It became infected. I had a lot of public appearances immediately after that race, meaning that I was spending the day walking around in dress shoes, not sitting with the foot elevated and recovering. I cleaned the wound with alcohol when I could, but with so many appearances the area remained moist, allowing infection to spread. The infection settled between layers of skin. The smell whenever I was able to air out the foot was atrocious.

As I said, the short time between New York and the Trials didn't really concern me. I was in fantastic shape heading into New York. All I needed to do before the Trials was rest a bit after New York, then do a few key workouts and long runs to bring that fitness back.

The same strategy can be used by all runners who want to capitalize on the hard work they did training for a marathon. If you take it easy in the one to two weeks after your marathon, you'll get revived physically and mentally. Then, assuming you came out of your marathon with nothing more than the usual short-term stiffness, you can soon chase another goal. That could be another marathon, but it doesn't have to be. Many elite runners do a spring marathon, recover quickly, and then have a phenomenal summer track season. They're really strong from marathon training. When they add in more speed work, they're ready to run faster than ever for 5K or 10K. You could be, too. Also, having another goal lined up relatively soon after one marathon can help you avoid that what-now post-marathon letdown.

So I didn't panic when my foot first got infected. At the Olympic Trials, all I had to do was finish in the top three. Not to discount my competitors, but I didn't feel I had to be in absolute peak shape to make the team. It would probably take 2:09 or 2:10 to finish in the top three. There were only a handful of guys, including me, running the Trials who had done so or had shown the potential to do so. I had just run 2:07 marathon pace for 21 miles. In terms of fitness, I was where I needed to be.

What worried me was whether my foot could go the distance. The infection lingered. Not only was I not running, I wasn't even walking normally. The Sport Center at Mammoth Hospital did everything they could to help me get back to training. At one point Dr. Mike Karch, head of the orthopedic department, told me, "We have to have you step on the foot. You have to start putting weight on it now. You won't be able to protect it in the race." I put on a snow boot with a Dr. Scholl's pad under the wound—the foot couldn't handle weight-bearing in normal footwear—and did a two-mile walk from the hospital. It was the most exercise I'd had in weeks.

I didn't resume running until thirty-eight days before the Trials. I started with a 30-minute run on pavement. A softer surface would have felt better on the foot, but I didn't want to risk dirt seeping into the infection. I was able to progress pretty quickly (thanks to that huge bank of fitness I already had). My longest runs between New York and the Trials were 17.5, 22, and 26.2 miles, the last one done on Christmas Day, twenty days before the Trials. That marathon-distance run was special because I did it with a brother in Christ, Brian Ball, who brought his fiancée and mom to help us with hydration and a ride back afterward. I did a lot of my runs with Brian. There were moments on our runs when I told Brian I needed to switch to the other side of the road or trail because the slanted surface was irritating my foot. Too bad I couldn't have that kind of command in races!

HAMMERING IN HOUSTON

Ryan Hall, winner of the previous Olympic Trials, had the fastest qualifying time. He was the favorite. You'll remember that he won the 2008 Trials by starting slowly and running the second half of the race much faster than the first. I knew that wouldn't be the case this time. Ryan had made no secret that he intended to start fast and see who was willing to go with him. He was the only one in the field who had run under 2:08. I knew I was capable of running that fast, so I told myself, "If he goes hard I'm going with him and will hang on for dear life."

I wasn't worried about my fitness. I was worried about how my foot was going to handle a fast-from-the-get-go on the hard streets of Houston. Much of the course was on the Allen Parkway, made of concrete, which is harder than asphalt. The skin was still raw, like baby skin. I extensively Vaselined the whole foot, even between my toes (and I made sure my Breathe Right strip was on my nose). Sure, I'd done a marathon-length run three weeks before. But that was at a moderate pace, in cushioned training shoes, and not pushing off as vigorously.

We weren't three steps into the race when Ryan did exactly what he said he would. Decision already made—go. By the 2nd mile there were seven of us in the lead pack: Ryan, Dathan Ritzenhein, Abdi Abdirahman, Mo Trafeh, Joseph Chirlee, Brian Olinger, and me. I knew what Dathan and Abdi could do. Dathan had placed ninth in the 2008 Olympics, ahead of Ryan, while Abdi was a three-time Olympian who knew how to peak when it mattered. I wasn't sure about the others. Trafeh and Olinger had qualified with times from shorter races, and Chirlee had a 2:18 personal best. I told myself the chance that they were all going to hang with this pace long enough to be a factor was small.

I also dealt with one of the stranger race-day incidents of my career. In training, I drink a small amount of coffee before long runs, interval workouts, and tempo runs. The caffeine gives me a physical and mental boost. Soon before races I take caffeine in pill form, because I don't want to risk the stomach problems coffee can cause. In Houston I learned that caffeine pills can cause their own problem—namely, the pill can get lodged in your throat. That was my situation as we set out at 2:06 marathon pace. I tried to either swallow or cough up the pill, but it was stuck. I thought back to New York City just two months earlier. There I'd set a personal best despite a Breathe Right strip in my shoe and having to stop several times to vomit. If I could succeed against those odds, I told myself, I could manage the pill-in-throat issue.

RUN TO WIN

A little after the 20-kilometer mark Abdi started to push into the lead. I thought, "It's okay, let him go." Coach Joe Vigil always talked about the nine inches above the shoulders being the most important part of racing. This was definitely a thinking-first race for me. I took it minute by minute, mile by mile, always considering what I should be doing in that moment to maximize my chance of finishing in the top three.

We passed halfway in just over 1:03, by far the fastest first-half split in Olympic Trials history. I took note of the time but didn't make much of it—I was comfortable and focused on competing. If there had been seven or eight others in the lead pack at that point, and someone started surging, I might have been in trouble. But the group was down to five; Chirlee and Olinger had lost contact before 10 miles. At this pace, there was little risk of someone catching us from behind. Only four of us in that five-man pack were proven marathoners. I needed to beat only two of the others to make the team. It was unlikely that three guys not named Keflezighi would hold that pace to the end. I told myself to tuck in, be smart, erase thoughts of blowing up, and believe that I could run 2:07 if that was what was necessary to make the team today.

About 70 minutes into the race, Ryan and Abdi started pushing the pace again and got a few steps ahead of Dathan and me. I was running the tangents—26.2 miles is plenty long—and noticed that they weren't. Around that time Dathan slipped and almost fell as we took a turn. These observations told me those guys were getting tired and either not thinking clearly or, in Dathan's case, getting sloppy mechanically. I smiled inside. They were all vulnerable. Trafeh was starting to lose contact. (He dropped out not long after.) I was fine staying behind and staying focused.

In the 18th mile, Dathan lost one, then two seconds to Ryan, Abdi, and me. I had earlier told Ryan that Dathan seemed to be hurting. Abdi, meanwhile, was raising his arms to get the crowd riled up as he surged again to a slight lead. I was still thinking Ryan looked the best.

The 20-mile mark is usually a significant point in the marathon; it was especially so this time. Dathan was now more than 10 seconds behind. He wouldn't have let that gap grow if he could help it. Ryan, Abdi, and I ran our 20th mile in 5:00, the slowest of the race. I was competing for place, not time, but this split gave me more evidence that Ryan was hurting. He loved to run as hard as possible for as long as possible. His pace slowing at this point wasn't a tactical decision to rest up for a hard last 5K; that wasn't Ryan's style. Also, a little past 20 miles I was finally able to cough up that caffeine pill. I started to sense that the day could be mine. "If the opportunity presents itself," I told myself, "move late, and move hard."

Ryan, Abdi, and I continued running together the next few miles as Dathan fell farther behind. We three would be the team. Now it was time to sort out our places. Abdi was the first to break, losing six seconds on Ryan and me in the 24th mile. I thought, "Here is my chance to win the Olympic Trials." Just after the 24-mile mark I did what Alan Culpepper had done to me eight years earlier, and what I'd done to win New York in 2009: I ran the next 400 meters as hard as I could. If I could build a big enough lead in that minute or so, I could settle back to the pace we'd been running, and Ryan would have to work twice as hard to catch back up. At the last aid station, with a little more than a mile to go, I took a quick look back. Ryan wasn't closing the gap.

It was a beautiful thing to come into those last 800 meters, with all the spectators there and some of the female competitors on the multi loop course clapping for me as I passed them.

I found someone in the crowd with a small American flag and grabbed it for the run in. In the final straight I could see I would be close to Ryan's Trials record of 2:09:02, but I didn't care about that. I was waving the flag and pumping my fist and saluting the Marines and otherwise celebrating the win and making the team. I was also thinking that Yohana's second birthday was in a few days, and how special it was to have her there with my parents and the rest of our family. The last 100 meters was a victory lap—not just for that race but for overcoming all of the physical and professional hardships since the previous Olympic Trials.

I finished in 2:09:08, a five-second improvement on the PR I'd set just two months earlier. Ryan finished second, 22 seconds behind me. Abdi was able to hold off a hard-charging Dathan. The four of us broke 2:10, making this the overall fastest Trials marathon in U.S. history. I was beyond psyched to make my third Olympic team, be the oldest Olympic Trials winner in history, and be the first track and field athlete to qualify for the 2012 Games. To not only win, but to do so in a shoe I'd helped develop and that bore my name, was incredible. Now it was time to see how close I could get to matching my silver-medal performance of eight years earlier.

2012 OLYMPIC MARATHON
(London, England)

AUGUST 12, 2012

PLACE **4th**   TIME   **2:11:06**

KEY LESSON

Go into races and other important situations with a series of goals that will keep motivating you to do your best.

My third time at the Olympics was one of the most satisfying races of my career. At age thirty-seven, I finished fourth against the world's best marathoners in a field that included the winner of the last two world championships, the second-fastest marathoner in history at the time, and the three fastest men of the year. Before the race, I had been considering retiring from professional running at the 2013 New York City Marathon. After the race, I was newly convinced I could still beat anyone in the world on the right day, including at the Boston Marathon.

On a personal level, my performance that day in London is one of the races I'm most proud of. Before the halfway mark I was in 21st place and on the verge of dropping out. I used every bit of mental tenacity I had to go from that low point to fourth place at the finish. I said in Chapter 13 that I dug deeper to finish fifth in the 2010 Boston Marathon than I had to win New York five months earlier. On the rare days when everything clicks, your main mental task is making good decisions, not willing yourself to overcome hardship. It's usually on the really rough days that you need to draw on all of your psychological strengths.

I had one of those days at the 2012 Olympics. I succeeded that day thanks to a mental technique that is just as useful in everyday life as it is in running.

BE MOTIVATED, NOT DEMORALIZED

Here's the gist of the technique: Go into tasks with a series of goals. Start with your dream outcome as your A goal. Then create a series of cascading backup goals that will also motivate you. When doing the task, try your absolute best to reach that dream goal. If it becomes obvious you won't reach that goal that day, refocus on reaching your B goal. As necessary, continue to move through your goals so that you keep working hard toward the best possible outcome rather than giving up.

In Chapter 12, I listed the key elements of any good goal. I said that the most important aspect of any goal is that it's personally meaningful to you, because then it will motivate you more than if it's a goal someone else set for you. Each of the goals you set for a race or another important task should have that characteristic. Then, when the going gets tough, you'll find a way to persevere.

What does this technique look like in practice? Let's say you have a 5K race this weekend. Your top goal could be to set a personal best. That will certainly motivate you to keep pushing in the final mile! But what happens if, in the 2nd mile, you realize you won't be running that fast? If your only goal for the race is to set a PR, you might give up—what's the point in continuing to suffer if you know you're going to come up short? You'll then finish the race much slower than you're capable of on that day, and feel that much more demoralized.

What's better in this scenario than a PR-or-bust outlook is to have those backup goals. Your B goal might be to run faster for 5K than you have in the past year. If that goal appears out of reach, then you shift your focus to your C goal, which could be something like running your 3rd mile within 10 seconds of your 1st mile. And so on, perhaps ending with the goal of finishing the race feeling like you gave your best effort under the circumstances. You can see how this series of goals will keep giving you reasons to be the best you. It's a "glass is half full" approach that helps you find the positives in difficult situations.

My upbringing was a key source of this mind-set. As a child I had chores such as fetching water or firewood. In the barren areas of Eritrea, it was often difficult to find all that we needed for daily life. I always set out with the goal of fulfilling my mother's request, such as getting a full basket of firewood. But that wasn't always possible. Sometimes I could find only enough to fill the bucket three-quarters full, or half full. I still worked as hard as I could to forage the next-best amount. Sometimes I couldn't find any wood. Then I would switch to finding cow, oxen, or donkey dung for heating fuel. My mother knew that whatever I returned home with, I had given 110 percent but wasn't always able to do what I had set out to do. I hope I lived up to that expectation during my marathon career. Most runners respect me for finishing a race when faced with challenges, instead of dropping out and getting ready for the next race.

Coach Larsen taught me how to apply this practice to running when I arrived at UCLA. When I was a freshman, we would sit down before big races and talk about goals and strategies.

He would say, "Obviously we'd love you to win. But you're only a freshman, and you'll be running against guys who have an edge on you in terms of age and experience. Finishing third and scoring those points for the team is better than going for the win no matter what and finishing worse than you could."

You can see in previous chapters how I used cascading goals in the 2004, 2008, and 2012 Olympic Marathon Trials. I entered each wanting to win; Coach Larsen always told me, "Show no mercy." In 2004 and 2012, I fought to meet that goal right up to the finish, taking first in 2012 and second in 2004. In the tough race I had at the 2008 Trials, when I couldn't cover Ryan Hall's second-half surge to the lead, I switched to my B goal, which was making the Olympic team by placing in the top three. When that result was no longer possible, I fought as hard as I could to stay in fourth, the alternate spot on the team. As the day became more difficult, I focused on simply reaching the finish line. Doing so was still a form of victory, given that I was running on a fractured pelvis.

Your range of goals during a race or other task can also become increasingly ambitious as events unfold. As I noted in the previous chapter, at the 2012 Olympic Trials I was focused on finishing in the top three for most of the race. Only after the 20-mile mark did my thinking really shift to winning.

If ever there was a race where I set higher goals as the miles accumulated, it was the London Olympic Marathon.

ROUGH START, TOUGH FINISH

My buildup for what I thought would be my final Olympics was good but not great. At age thirty-seven, I was finding it harder to hold up to the marathon training schedule that had brought me so much success over the previous decade. Eventually I made some changes that helped me thrive into my forties; I'll detail those in Chapter 23. But going into the London Games, a few injuries meant that I stood on the start line a few weeks shy of peak fitness.

To be honest, I also stood on the start line a little miffed. There were 105 of us in the field. The public announcer introduced a handful of runners, such as two-time world champion Abel Kirui and his teammate Wilson Kipsang, whose best of 2:03:42 was the fastest in the field (and at the time made him the second-fastest in history). He didn't introduce me. I was the only Olympic Marathon medalist in the field, had won the world's largest marathon, and was the American Olympic Trials champion. Instead, they introduced my teammate Ryan Hall. How about a little love for a thirty-seven-year-old still going strong? I tucked the slight away, to draw on for some I'll-show-you inspiration later on.

With guys like Kipsang and three young Ethiopians who had broken 2:05 that year in the field, I figured the pace would be fast from the start. My plan was to let the leaders go, run in the chase pack, and then pick off as many of the front-runners as possible in the second half of the race. My A goal was another medal; my B goal was a top-ten finish.

Things got interesting almost immediately. At one of the early aid stations, I was given Ryan's bottle instead of mine. This was not a good development. I can see how someone might have mistaken me for our teammate Abdi Abdirahman, who was also born in East Africa. But Ryan? He's white and blond; I'm black and bald.

A little background: Customized fluids are one of the benefits of being an elite marathoner. In training, we can find which drink works best for us, and then have that available in bottles we provide for the aid stations, which typically appear every 5K. The flip side of having access to your own tried-and-true drink is that mistakes happen—you might be in a tight pack and, while running at 12 miles per hour, not be able to navigate over to the table where your bottle is. Or, as occurred here, you might be given someone else's bottle. (The 2012 Games included a new policy in which runners were handed bottles by someone from their country.) In that situation, you have to decide whether your need for fluids outweighs the risk of breaking the cardinal rule of not trying anything new on race day.

Ryan and I were good friends. I knew how important his drinks were to him. He was behind me, already struggling with the hamstring issue that would lead to his eventually dropping out. I slowed until he caught me and gave him his bottle. Unfortunately, he hadn't been given mine. Ryan drank from his bottle, then handed it to me and said to finish it. With an 11 a.m. start, we would be running in the hottest, sunniest part of the day. I needed fluids. I downed the rest of Ryan's drink and hoped for the best.

Pretty soon my stomach started cramping. The always-tender spot on the ball of my left foot was developing a blister, probably from the cobblestones we occasionally ran over. I lost contact with the chase pack and began to be caught by others. At one point I was in 21st place, and going the wrong way through the field for someone with hopes for a medal.

The thought "Drop out" flashed across my mind at the Cathedral. I was already scheduled for New York, less than three months away. The hurting part of me reasoned that the best course of action was to call it a day and try again in November. I already had my Olympic medal. What did I have to prove to anyone?

As usually happens in these situations, I was able to challenge those thoughts. I recalled saying after winning the Trials in January that we were sending the best possible marathon team. How would it look if the winner of that race then dropped out on the biggest stage in sport? What kind of lesson would that be to my daughters and the fifty-plus other family members and friends who had made the trip to London with me? What about my fans, both those on hand and watching around the world? Plus, I was wearing the USA jersey for what I thought would be the last time. I needed to represent our country to the best of my ability. I also thought about all the people who would love to be in my shoes, running the Olympic Marathon. So, much earlier in the race than would be ideal, I went through my cascading list of goals and settled on what's usually my when-all-else-fails resolution: Whatever it takes, get to the finish line.

That commitment helped me regroup and refocus. If I was going to finish, then I should try to run with others to make the miles less daunting. I prayed for strength. I was able to latch back onto the rear of the chase pack. I passed the halfway point in 17th place. Now that I had weathered the earlier crisis, my competitive instincts began to return. I told myself, "Try to beat at least one of these guys." I started feeling a little better. I thought, "Try to beat two of them."

And so it continued the next several miles—as my situation improved, so did my outlook, and my goals became more ambitious. Others fell out of the chase pack. At 30 kilometers, I was in tenth place. It looked like I would reach one of my pre-race goals after all, of finishing in the top ten. So why not try to finish as high up in the top ten as possible?

Before the 20-mile mark, a Japanese runner, Kentaro Nakamoto, surged. I latched on. I hoped he would pull me through more of the field, and that I'd pass him just before the finish. I spent the next few miles staring at his back, willing myself not to lose contact, even though we were so tired we weren't running the tangents. I reminded myself that every step took us closer to the finish and the redemption I'd feel there for having overcome my earlier urge to drop out.

At 37 kilometers, with just more than 3 miles to run, I saw Coach Larsen hold out six fingers. I'd lost count. I didn't know if it meant I was in sixth place or Nakamoto was in sixth place. (It turned out I was.) Then I saw a green jersey up ahead. I started doing the math in my head: "If I'm in sixth, then the green jersey is in fourth. Who knows, maybe one of the medalists will fail a drug test and be stripped of his medal. If I can catch the green jersey, there's a slight chance I could be a medalist again!"

With just more than a kilometer to go, someone from the crowd yelled, "You can get the next guy!" I nodded my head in acknowledgment and started to charge forward.

(I eventually got to meet my encourager, Phil Racht, who had come from Atlanta to watch me and the rest of the marathoners run. He became a MEB Foundation runner and a friend.)

I passed the runner in the green jersey, two-time New York City Marathon champion Marilson Gomes dos Santos, with 500 meters to go. I was so excited about how I'd gone from almost dropping out to finishing fourth that as I approached the finish line and saw a spectator with an American flag, I grabbed it and ran with it above my head to the finish. Maybe only the winner is supposed to do this. But I felt like I'd had a huge personal victory, thanks to constant internal communication and goal assessment as the race unfolded.

I didn't win a medal that day, but I learned so much. I dug deeper than ever for a solid finish. Many veterans of the sport have told me it was a bigger accomplishment than my silver medal. I learned to never give up on a race, no matter how challenging it gets. Think about the others involved in your running, like I thought about the importance of representing my family, community, and country. You'll get a new perspective. That fourth-place finish reopened the door to the Boston Marathon and left me optimistic for the future.

PLACE **23rd**   TIME   **2:23:47**

KEY LESSON

You never know who you're going to touch and what you're going to learn about yourself when faced with adversity.

One of the great things about marathoning compared to other sports is that pros and everyday practitioners compete on the same course at the same time. What better way to symbolize that we marathoners all experience the same joys and challenges? I love the spirit of common humanity on marathon day.

Throughout my career I strove to emphasize the common bond among all runners, regardless of pace. In Chapter 14 I talked about how social media has allowed me to connect with so many fellow runners I otherwise would never meet. Doing so helps to break down the artificial barrier some people erect between elite and recreational runners. Connecting with others helps everyone realize that, whether you run a marathon in two or four or six hours, there will be tough days. Where we can learn from one another is in how we handle those tough days.

There was plenty to learn during and after the 2013 New York City Marathon, the slowest of my career.

RECLAIMING RUNNING

I was feeling a little beat up heading into that year's marathon. I suffered a tear of the left soleus, one of the calf muscles, in September. I was coming back from that injury when, later that month, I fell hard onto an unfinished road, with gravel protruding from the surface, one mile into a planned 10-miler. My knee was gashed so deeply that I could see the white fat layer. It was bleeding profusely. I made a U-turn for home. The knee remained stiff and sometimes hard to bend for most of the rest of my buildup. The longest run I was able to get in was 20 miles, much shorter than the 25 miles or longer I prefer to peak at. I wasn't sure if I could go the distance at race pace. At one point I discussed not starting with Coach Larsen as well as the race organizers, the New York Road Runners.

The thing is, marathoning was also feeling a little beat up. Hurricane Sandy had led to the cancellation of the previous year's New York City Marathon. Then came the horrific bombings near the finish line of the 2013 Boston Marathon. The 2013 New York City Marathon would be a chance to reestablish running as a public celebration of the positive values of sport. It was really important to me to be part of that celebration. (I wasn't alone in that feeling—50,266 people completed the race, the first time in history a marathon had more than 50,000 finishers.)

I knew my body was fragile. I knew I wasn't in shape to contend for the win. But I decided I would put myself in the thick of it and see what happened.

ONE STEP AT A TIME

Race day was chilly and windy. There would be no rush of guys finishing under 2:10 as there had been two years earlier, the last time the race was run. There would, however, be stiff competition. Course record holder Geoffrey Mutai of Kenya was back, as was Tsegaye Kebede of Ethiopia, third in that record-breaking race of 2011. The reigning Olympic and world champion, Stephen Kiprotich of Uganda, was also on hand.

I was able to run with the leaders through about 16 miles, just before we entered Manhattan for the traditional increase in pace on First Avenue. I fell farther behind when the surging started. What usually happens is that the pace then settles back down for a few miles. I thought if I pushed hard I could regain contact with the lead pack and get pulled along at least until we reached Central Park. I dug down deep and tried to close the gap.

My give-it-a-go strategy got the best of me. Whereas at the 2004 Olympic Trials, I took a shot despite compromised preparation and finished wondering, "Where did that come from?," this time it was like, "You knew you weren't ready, and here's the proof." At the 19.2-mile mark, disaster struck. All of a sudden my right hip flexors stopped working. There was just no way I could take the next step. My mind said "go" and my body said "no." I have felt the excitement of winning races; it can be such a beautiful thing that you don't want to stop running. This experience was the complete opposite. I stopped. My mind and body had an awkward moment where they weren't on the same page.

Although I had discussed not starting, I never seriously considered dropping out. I thought about all the people who would love to have the opportunity in front of me: those who had come from all over the world to run New York in 2012, only for the race to be canceled; those who were prevented from finishing Boston that spring because of the bombings; those who applied to but didn't get entry into New York that year; those who love to run but for whatever reason aren't able to do marathons. Also, my dad's journey to escape Eritrea during the war with Ethiopia came to mind. He didn't have aids like fluids and gels, whereas I could get fluids the rest of the way. That put things in perspective. I told myself, "I know what it's like to win. Now I'm going to find out what it's like to get to the finish line no matter what, even if I have to walk the last seven miles."

My 20th mile took almost 10 minutes—twice the time of most of the previous miles, and not too far off my 5K PR of 13:11! When the hip flexor issue arose, I stopped for at least 30 seconds. Then I got going again, *slowly*, only to have to stop again. I had a vision of the elite runners' sweep van coming to pick me up, and me needing to convince them I was going to finish. Even with wearing arm warmers, gloves, and a hat in addition to my singlet and shorts, I was already starting to get cold, now that I was running so much slower than my race pace. The warmth and blankets in the sweep van did cross my mind.

I probably stopped at least seven times. I don't know for sure because I lost count after a while. I would stop and walk for the simple reason that my body couldn't keep running. I would stop for 5 seconds, 10 seconds, whatever it took until I felt like I could get going again. I tried to stay positive, telling myself I was closer to the finish than I was the last time I'd stopped. I'd resume running at a shuffle and gradually get to a faster pace, but one still far from what I'd usually be hitting at that point in a marathon.

Mike Cassidy, a Staten Island resident, caught up to me with about 5K to go. Mike and I had just met that morning before the start. Our conversation then was brief. When I told Mike I'd see him out there on the course, he had replied I'd be way ahead of him. Usually, he would have been correct, given his personal best of 2:18.

But this was an unusual day, for both of us. As Mike pulled alongside me, he said, "Let's go, Meb." I said, "I'll try," just as I did when the other elite runners who passed during my frequent stops encouraged me to join them. I was able to match his pace. I was running on pure instinct now, knowing without ever having to consider it that someone by my side would make the last few miles much easier. I turned to Mike and said, "Let's finish this together." Mike agreed, even though he could have easily pulled away from me.

I'm pretty sure I didn't stop once Mike and I started running together. On the most rolling part of the course, on the east side of Central Park, I would tell Mike when I'd be slowing, which was usually on the uphills. He would encourage me to focus on just getting to the top of the hill. The downhills weren't as bad, because I didn't need to lift my legs as much. I focused on leaning forward and letting gravity do some of the work.

As we reentered Central Park at Columbus Circle for the final 600 meters, Mike turned to me and said, "It's an honor to run with you." I replied, "Today is not about us. It's about representing New York. It's about representing Boston. It's about representing the USA and doing something positive for our sport. We will finish this race holding hands."

Which we did, our arms raised high. The official results show Mike finishing twenty-second in 2:23:46 and me placing twenty-third in 2:23:47. Figuratively, I can't imagine that two runners ever finished a marathon closer than Mike and I did.

THE CAMARADERIE OF COMPETITION

After the race I was very emotional. I limped into the media center and repeatedly paused to cry while answering questions. Many people took this to mean I was upset about my result.

That wasn't the case. As I mentioned in Chapter 7, I never had a race in my life that afterward I thought was worth a cry over disappointment. It was more what Mike said and realizing what our run together meant to him. I didn't realize while it was happening that it would impact him the way it did. To me, Mike was a peer. We were just working hard together to get to the finish line. I was just a fellow runner.

That's the beauty of our sport. Like I said, we had just met that morning, and only briefly, through Dr. Andy Rosen, a mutual friend who heads up the race's medical team for invited runners. I didn't really know anything about Mike—what his political views are, what his religion is, anything like that. I just knew him as Mike Cassidy the runner, a local guy good enough to start up front. He turned out to be a great guy who I've stayed in touch with and try to see and run with when I'm in New York. He eventually became a teammate with the New York Athletic Club and a contributor to my foundation. But at the time, it was all about two runners on a journey together, and I enjoyed it as much as he did.

Reflecting on those last few miles with Mike really drove home for me the deep bond that exists among runners. We all know it's hard and that it hurts. If it were easy, everybody and their mother would do it. Those of us who have run a marathon have that special respect for the distance, and that mutual respect for anyone who reaches the finish line.

Even though I trained a lot on my own, especially for the last phase of my career, I always loved the company of my teammates, and even of my rivals. After 20 or 23 miles, if I'm running next to someone, of course I want to win—and so does he. But there's no malice in those thoughts. We all want to help each other do the best we can.

You see the same in many sports, and many nonsport endeavors, where success requires endless hours of preparation and the rewards are mostly internal. At track and field meets, watch the field event athletes congratulate each other after the competition to see what I mean. There's that mutual respect because you know what lies behind the other's performance, regardless of how "good" or "bad" it is. Watching someone finish a marathon, you know from your own experience what it took to get there: all those mornings when you overcame the temptation to sleep in rather than run; all those long runs where you willed yourself to keep moving, and were glad afterward you did; all those times you headed out the door in search of the best you. We have far more important things in common than might be indicated by finishing a number of minutes or hours apart from each other.

My race in New York really drove home how you can inspire others on a day that wasn't your best. In my next marathon I'd learn what could happen in that regard on your day of days.

2014 BOSTON MARATHON

APRIL 21, 2014

PLACE **1st**   TIME   **2:08:37**

KEY LESSON

We all have our day when everything clicks. If you recognize when it's happening, you can produce something that's bigger than yourself.

Two nights before the 2014 Boston Marathon, I was walking from the Harvard Club with race director Dave McGillivray after meeting with the Martin Richard Foundation and many charity teams, including the MEB Foundation. Dave asked me, "What's your goal for Monday?" I said, "To win. I'm going to go for it."

Of course I always ran to win, in the sense of getting the best out of myself on race day. But this time was different—I meant it literally. Boston 2014 was a special focus long before I broke the tape on Boylston Street.

SETTING THE GOAL

I had watched the 2013 Boston Marathon from a grandstand by the finish with my good friend from San Diego, Rob Hill. Injury had scuttled my plan to be there as a competitor. While I would have liked to be racing, watching thousands of runners finish amid the palpable positive energy was a great experience. I was taking photos and notes on the positive humanity and camaraderie the marathon embraces. It had been thirty years since an American man won Boston. As soon as Lelisa Desisa of Ethiopia broke the tape in 2:10:22, I texted my friend and fellow U.S. Olympian Ryan Hall, who also missed the race because of injury. "WE CAN DO THIS," implying winning next year, I wrote. Ryan texted back almost immediately, "We'll get after it." Already fired up for 2014, I left the stands.

Then came the bombings. One of the explosions happened right in front of where I'd been sitting. Like the rest of the running community and the world, I couldn't process this senseless act. Marathons bring out the best of the human spirit: pushing yourself to accomplish more than you thought possible; working with others toward mutually meaningful goals; erasing barriers of race, age, gender, nationality, and creed. And they do so in a peaceful, joy-filled atmosphere. Why would someone turn the site of a celebration of all that's good about humanity into a scene of death and destruction?

Early that evening Bonnie Ford of ESPN asked me if I planned to come back to the marathon. Would I be scared to race on the streets of Boston? Would I bring my family? I said that I hoped to be healthy enough to win the marathon for the people of Boston. The tragedy of the bombings elevated the importance of my original goal. I would be racing not just for myself but to be part of the process of healing and redemption.

I already sensed that the 2014 Boston Marathon could be one of running's greatest days. I wanted to play an important role in it.

When you make a statement like that, you're committing yourself. Still, saying that my goal was to win Boston in 2014 was an example of the "underpromise and overdeliver" philosophy I described in Chapter 3. Besides talking with Bonnie on the night of the bombings and with Dave McGillivray a year later, I told very few people about my goal. One other instance came in November 2013, when Jonny Gomes and Jarrod Saltalamacchia of the Boston Red Sox placed the World Series trophy on the marathon finish line. I told a friend I wanted to inspire that same feeling of resilience and reclamation by winning on Patriots' Day.

The sense of accountability I felt was primarily to myself. I did a lot of visualization of running Boston. In bed and at other calm, quiet times I would imagine myself on various parts of the course, running hard with good form and cadence. I pictured myself coming down Boylston Street in the lead. I did the same on runs. At home in San Diego, I trained in Mission Bay Park. Returning home from the park entails running uphill, then a right turn, followed by a left turn. I ran this stretch visualizing myself making the right turn on Hereford Street, then the left turn on Boylston that defines the last half mile of the Boston course. The visualizations were so strong that I felt like I was on Boylston. I would cross myself twice at different times, to mark where the two bombs exploded. At rest and while running I prayed, "God, help me make that dream come true."

The pre-race period was like before my win in New York in 2009, in that I had a special feeling and drive for the race. It was unlike before New York in that I didn't show up on the line in phenomenal shape.

I had started the year strong with a win at the Houston Half

Marathon in 1:01:23, only 23 seconds off the PR I set a month before winning New York. I was seeing good results from switching my training from a seven-day to a nine-day cycle. This change allowed me, at age thirty-eight, to get in more recovery after my long runs, tempo runs, and interval workouts. (I'll discuss this approach more in Chapter 23.) But despite the additional recovery, I was battling a hamstring strain by March. At the NYC Half Marathon, five weeks before Boston, I ran conservatively, placing tenth in 1:02:53. I needed to protect the hamstring. Everything was pointing to April 21 in Boston. I didn't run the day after the half marathon, and I took another day off on April 10 because my right quad felt weak and sore.

The night before the marathon, I told Yordanos, "This is it, my last shot at a Boston Marathon title." But I wasn't desperate. I thought about the Eminem line: "One shot, or one opportunity / To seize everything you ever wanted."

The only thing missing from my running résumé was a Boston title. I felt I could do it by drawing on the spirit of the thirty-six thousand other runners who would be out there taking back the streets of Boston. Before the race I wondered how best to honor the victims. Have a picture of the four fatalities under my bib and pull it out at the end of the race? Write their names on my bib? As an elite, this isn't an easy decision, because the sponsors get very protective of their image and want to make sure it shows on the bib. I took a medium risk: Write their names on my bib with a Sharpie so that they'd be visible, but not as big as I would have liked to.

On race morning, I chilled out in the church in Hopkinton where the pros are based before the race. Former New York City Marathon race director Mary Wittenberg took a photo of me from the second floor because she couldn't believe how relaxed I looked. I was at peace. There are no guarantees in the marathon or life. I reminded myself that all I could do was control what

I could. I knew the crowds would be amazing and that the day would be very emotional. I wanted to calm myself before the race and then draw on all that energy once the gun went off.

Coach Larsen had always believed I could run 2:07 or 2:08 on the course. If he'd said that before my two other Bostons, in 2006 and 2010, I'd have believed it. But this time, I wasn't so sure. He reminded me I'd run 2:09:56 in 2006 when I went out too fast and 2:09:26 in 2010 with a ruptured quad. I told Bob not to worry if he didn't see me on TV early on. "If you're going to see me, it will be in the last 5K," I said. "Before that I won't even be in the picture."

THE NINE INCHES ABOVE THE SHOULDERS ARE THE MOST IMPORTANT

My main goal was to win. My backup goals were to place in the top three or set a personal best. Winning or placing on the podium didn't require immediate action once the race started. Setting a PR, however, meant that I needed to make sure the early pace was honest. I was raring to go and was at the front almost immediately. I wasn't pushing the pace aggressively at that point, just making sure I gave myself my best shot at meeting my goals.

The field certainly had the ability to run fast the whole way. Last year's winner, Lelisa Desisa of Ethiopia, was back. Dennis Kimetto of Kenya, second-fastest in the world the previous year, was touted by many to be the favorite. (Later in 2014 he became the first to break 2:03 with his 2:02:57 world record in Berlin.) I started the race with the 15th best PR in the field. But I'd shown time and again, especially on challenging courses without pacers, that I could run with anyone.

Desisa, Kimetto, and the rest of the lead pack showed no interest in running fast at that point. Ryan Hall took a brief turn at the lead and then drifted back. At around mile 5, I realized the Kenyans and Ethiopians were trying to slow the pace. I was in the lead, and none of the big names were there with me. Moving ahead at this point against a field of that caliber was an extremely risky move. I had a sudden inner vision that it was the right thing to do. I strongly believe there was a higher purpose at play that day, that the stars were all aligned for me. This was the moment I had prayed for. It was important to seize that opportunity.

Josphat Boit, a former teammate from the Mammoth Track Club, left the pack and joined me. Josphat is a native of Kenya who ran at the University of Arkansas. It was amazing to have two naturalized U.S. citizens leading the Boston Marathon on this day. No matter how the rest of the race turned out, we were doing our part to showcase the American dream.

Josphat soon gapped me a little bit. I told myself to let him have his space, that I didn't need to be competitive in that way this early. It was more efficient to gradually work my way back to Josphat. I figured the chase pack would soon catch up to us, so there was no point in rushing to close the gap with Josphat.

By mile 8, I was thinking differently. I'd broken away three miles earlier. The pack had had 15 minutes to catch up, and they didn't. I said to Josphat, "What are they thinking?" I couldn't believe it—my dream might be coming true.

In high school and college, I'd always been a front-runner. I became less of one when I moved up to the marathon. With energy conservation so important over 26.2 miles, there's usually little to gain from being in the lead early on. Still, I was used to running long and hard by myself. Over the previous few years I'd done almost all of my training on my own. Mentally, I was prepared to go hard the rest of the way without being in a pack. Josphat bumped into me. I made a mental note that he was getting tired. As Josphat and I continued to pull away, and then Josphat began to fall off the pace, I told myself, "There's nothing you can do to take it back." I was now committed to running from the front, solo, the rest of the way.

And really, at the end of the day, what did I have to lose? My previous marathon had been the slowest of my career. My thirty-ninth birthday was two weeks away. I thought I might be running my final Boston race. I was going to give it my all. If I lost, I'd be able to sleep soundly that night, with no regrets.

BOSTON STRONG, MEB STRONG

If you've run Boston you've probably noticed the big sign at 13.1 miles letting you know you've reached the halfway point, roughly where the famous Wellesley College scream tunnel is. I didn't see it in 2014, and I don't remember it now. Usually I'm very focused on splits, including landmark ones like halfway. That's good information to help guide your remaining miles and to see how your body is responding to your effort. This time, I was so in the zone that I ran right past the halfway marker.

Fifteen miles in, I was still running solo. The enormity of what was happening was starting to sink in. At my pace I had less than an hour to go. I thought, "If they're going to come, they're going to have to earn it." The phrase *Boston Strong* was visible everywhere that weekend, including on posters along and written on the roads of the course. I told myself, "Boston strong, Meb strong." I recognized the opportunity the day was providing. We runners work so hard to prepare for race day, but as you've already seen, there are so many little things that can go wrong—from a misplaced Breathe Right strip to a bottle mix-up. Once in a great while everything aligns, with our bodies operating at full capacity, and our minds in intimate, perfect sync with our actions. It's so important to recognize when this is happening and to have the courage to act on it.

For me that day in Boston, that meant it was time to really start pushing. It was time to throw caution to the wind and go for it. "If they catch me, they catch me," I thought. I ran the downhill 16th mile in 4:31. I was all by myself. I had never really run my own race in a marathon before. This time there was no initiating or reacting to the moves of others. I would dictate the pace. "It's all on me now," I thought. My strategy was straightforward—run as hard as I could for as long as I could and pray that it got me to the finish line first.

I took a long, long look back as I made the turn at the famed Newton Fire Station, a little bit past the 17-mile mark. The next turn on the course was in the final mile. So that turn at the fire station was my last chance to get a clear picture of what was happening behind me, unless I wanted to constantly turn around. At that point I knew Josphat was behind me, but I had no idea who else was coming. As I made the right for the approach to the Newton hills, I swiveled my head as far as I could, and I saw . . .

Nobody. Not the defending champ, not the one guy in the field with a 2:03 PR, not any of the other twelve guys with faster PRs than me. I didn't know how big my lead was, but I knew it wasn't small.

As someone who's usually the hunter rather than the hunted, I knew that the ones doing the chasing on a point-to-point course have better information on where they stand than the person up front. And they have each other to work with. The best thing for me to do was to work the hills as hard as possible. If they couldn't see me, they wouldn't know how hard to go to catch me. Checking my watch gave me confidence. If I had seen miles in the 5:20s, I would have thought, "Oh no, I've hit the Wall, they still have time to run me down." But I was still seeing miles around 5:00. The longer I could keep up that pace, the faster they'd have to push through the hills and over the last five miles to get me. I got another boost from realizing the 5:00 miles were still coming at a submaximal effort.

TAKING BACK BOSTON

Speaking of boosts: The crowds were going out of their minds seeing me alone in the lead. A lot of them probably had better information than I did on how far back the chase pack was. The usual chants of "USA! USA!" and "Go, Meb!" took on a much stronger meaning for all of us as the dream of an American winning Boston one year after the bombings came closer and closer to reality.

I tried to keep calm but couldn't help myself after cresting Heartbreak Hill. The energy was electric. I would spontaneously pump my fist or give a thumbs-up to a fan. I'd have to pull myself back to the task at hand. "Concentrate!" I told myself. "You can do that all you want once you get to the finish line."

My resolve to be all business sometimes wavered. At mile 23, I did a fist bump and snuck a quick look back. I saw an orange shirt. I had no idea who it was. I thought maybe it was Gebre Gebremariam of Ethiopia, the 2010 New York winner known for his great finishing speed. Whoever it was, he hadn't been visible the last time I'd looked. Translation: He was running faster than me, and we still had 5K to go.

All of the visualization I'd done in the months before the race had seeped into my subconscious. One night I had a dream of me and one other runner racing down Boylston Street to the finish. I never got to the part of the dream where one of us won. Now the same scenario might be playing out in real life.

The man behind me, who I later learned was Wilson Chebet of Kenya, kept closing. At mile 24, I entertained the thought of holding back to save energy for the last 600 meters on Boylston. Maybe I was thinking that because by now I was so tired, and my mind was trying to come up with ways to ease my suffering. The fighter in me took over. I told myself, "No, don't hold back now. Try to maintain or extend the gap." As you may have experienced, if you come from behind to catch another runner, especially late in the race, you have the mental edge. I drew on my experience to overcome the urge to relax a bit before a final push.

I had never been in such duress while leading a race. As I said in Chapter 12, it's often in the races you don't win that you dig down the deepest. When I won New York in 2009, I still had more left in me. But that wasn't the case this day in Boston. I was at my physical and mental limits. My old foot wound hurt each of the nearly 100 times per minute my left foot was on the ground. My body was tightening up all over, and the hamstring strain I'd finessed during my buildup was screaming. I was pushing so hard to maintain or extend the gap that I realized I was about to vomit. I couldn't vomit to the side or otherwise let Chebet see what was happening; he was now close enough that he'd be able to pick up on how much I was hurting. That would spur him to push even harder and exploit my vulnerability. I tilted my head back and swallowed my vomit.

At one point Chebet got the gap down to 6 seconds. That's about 40 yards at our marathon pace. I had to keep pressing. I told myself, "Focus, focus, focus. Mechanics, mechanics, mechanics." Concentrating on maintaining good running form took my mind off how much I was hurting and helped me keep up my pace. Doing a quick body scan to see if you can run more efficiently is a great way to get through late-race tough patches.

I got a huge mental boost when I realized Chebet had stopped gaining on me. "If he could catch me, he would," I thought. "He wouldn't want to wait around. He'd want to put me away." I was still hurting like I'd never hurt before, but I was now strengthened psychologically. I relied on the cheering crowds and the victims' angels to give me strength.

Then came the right on Hereford and the left on Boylston that I'd visualized so many times over the previous year. I crossed myself at the first bombing site, in honor of all the victims, especially the four fatalities. I took a good look back as I ran past the 26-mile mark and saw that Chebet wasn't closing. I pumped my right fist. I pumped my left fist. I nervously peeked back; Chebet still wasn't closing. I pumped both fists, raised my sunglasses to my forehead, and crossed myself again just before the finish at the site of the second bombing. I poured myself into the finish tape. I had won the Boston Marathon! I raised my arms and gave thanks to God. My dream had become a reality.

A WIN FOR EVERYONE

My arms were still raised to the heavens when Yordanos ran out and almost knocked me over with her embrace. It turned out to be an apt metaphor for the aftermath of my win. I was overwhelmed, in the best possible way, by the response to my victory.

I had hoped all along that my winning Boston in 2014 would resonate beyond hard-core running fans. Yes, I'd become the first American man since 1983 to take the title. And yes, I'd lowered my personal best by 31 seconds, to 2:08:37, two weeks before my thirty-ninth birthday. But what really mattered was that my win symbolized what we all did that day. Everybody was looking to do something positive, not for themselves, but for the city of Boston, the people of Boston, and the running community. We all wanted to show that we're resilient. We all wanted to celebrate the freedom we have to run 26.2 miles through the streets of one of the world's great cities. We all wanted to own Boylston Street and change the previous year's tragedy into something positive. We all ran to win that day. I just happened to get to the line first.

The next several days were a blur. The day after, I woke to see myself on the front pages of newspapers from around the world. President Obama called me to congratulate me and thank me for how I'd helped the race, the city, and the country heal. By the end of the week I still hadn't looked at my phone. A week and a half later I still hadn't been home. So many people wanted to hear my story and tell me their story about that magical day. But the magical day did come with a price—the old wound on my left foot. I had to drain it at least sixteen times. As I moved slowly and unbalanced for weeks, the wound was a constant reminder of why I was being feted with such an awesome celebration.

When you do something above and beyond the norm, you'll touch others. You might not get the immediate and widespread reaction I did with my victory, but you know that your accomplishments will register with others. My win in Boston gave me a much bigger platform than I'd ever had. As one friend put it, you're at a new level when you're a sports figure known by one name. You're also at a new level when strangers twice your age approach you and tell you you're their hero. With that honor comes great responsibility to handle it well. Wherever I went, I needed to be aware that I was an ambassador for running and much more. At the same time, the bigger platform didn't change the core of what I do day in and day out—using running as a way to inspire others to run to win in their own way.

After winning Boston, my résumé was complete. I could have retired from competitive running that day entirely satisfied. But I wanted to keep going. I simply loved running and racing too much to step away. Besides, I'd just set a PR! By continuing to run, and continuing to run to win, I hoped I could reach more people than ever.

2014 NEW YORK CITY MARATHON

NOVEMBER 2, 2014

PLACE   **4th**   TIME   **2:13:18**

KEY LESSON

Mother Nature and other forces outside your control will always be a factor, but you can't let them ruin your race.

How windy was the 2014 New York City Marathon? The wheelchair and handcycle athletes started in Brooklyn and raced 23.2 miles; it would have been too dangerous for them to start on Staten Island and cross the Verrazano-Narrows Bridge. Even when not crossing one of the world's longest suspension bridges, we dealt with winds of up to 40 miles per hour.

I like nice weather as much as anyone, but on the bus to the start that morning I was a little happy inside about the wind. On a day when a lot of runners were freaking out about the conditions, I considered the wacky weather an asset. I wasn't going to fight the wind, literally or figuratively. I was going to acknowledge and accept it as something outside my control, something that would affect everyone, and something that I could either waste mental energy on or use to my advantage. My finishing fourth against an amazing field after an abbreviated buildup shows what's possible when you focus on what you can control.

COMPETITIVE, NOT COMPLACENT

It's fair to say I didn't rush back into training after winning Boston. I would have taken a break from running for quite a while regardless of the result, because my old foot wound was a mess after the race. It took a long time to recover because of the unprecedented demands on my time after my victory. Don't get me wrong—it was an honor to be in such high demand in the days, weeks, even months after my win. People never seemed to tire of hearing the story of my win, and I never tired of telling it. It was immensely satisfying to connect with so many people, to make new friends and reacquaint myself with old ones. The downside of all those appearances was a lot of walking, sitting, and standing that prolonged swelling in the foot. Wearing dress shoes for my many formal events didn't help. I traveled with a first-aid kit so that I could clean the foot daily to keep it from getting infected. The wound was so severe I had to drain it with race bib pins and sewing kit needles. In all, the foot was drained sixteen times by professionals or me.

I did think about retiring after Boston. There's something compelling about going out on top. But I realized I just love running too much—the training, the racing, the fellowship, the simple pleasure of being fit—to stop just yet. I also wanted to use the bigger platform I now had to inspire that many more people to dream big, work hard, and strive to be the best they can be. One day I told Yordanos, "You know, the Olympics are only two years away. . . ." Sure, I'd be forty-one by the time of the marathon at the Rio Games. But I'd just won the world's most prestigious marathon two weeks before my thirty-ninth birthday. When you train and race in the clean and natural way, with the right motivation, you can sustain a given level of fitness for a long time. It wasn't like I'd done anything crazy or unrepeatable in my Boston preparation. I didn't see why I couldn't repeat that performance.

Even though I didn't retire after Boston, some people thought I'd be phoning it in at New York. I'd said winning Boston made my career checklist complete; why bother putting myself through all that pain again, especially since I'd already won New York? Why not enjoy the experience, run only as hard as I felt like, and let the young, hungry guys fight for the win?

It was really important to show that's not who I am. After I won Olympic silver in 2004, I tried as hard as I could to win New York seventy days later. After I won New York in 2009, I was more motivated than ever to win Boston the following April. These are the sorts of challenges I set for myself, where one success isn't an excuse for complacency but a building block to accomplishing more. I had surprised most of the running world by winning Boston. Wouldn't it be great to follow that up with another New York title? I was going to run to win in New York for my own internal satisfaction, and to be a good role model to the many new fans I made in Boston.

The foot wound and post-victory public appearances meant I got a late start on training for New York. Things really started to come together only when I escaped to Mammoth Lakes for altitude training for the four weeks before the marathon. I got in some solid tempo runs and two 26-mile long runs. Unlike before Boston, I had no bodily issues. On race day I was healthy but a little short on fitness.

AGAINST THE WIND

In the conditions we faced that day in New York, I wouldn't have struck out on my own regardless of whether I'd won Boston. That's not how you win marathons in a 30-miles-per-hour headwind. As in the Tour de France, the top contenders will let you go to expend huge amounts of energy on your own while they take turns drafting off one another before reeling you in. If you've run in a big city on a really windy day, you know that the wind is made worse by all the tall buildings. It slinks and swirls unpredictably; you'll be running into a headwind when all of a sudden a strong gust from the side will almost lift you off your feet. As we ran through Brooklyn, large pieces of trash occasionally blew across an avenue as if shot out of a cannon.

I wouldn't have had the option of an early solo break even on a calm day. My competitors weren't going to let me use that strategy two marathons in a row. My best bet was to tuck in and see how the race developed.

Nobody was going to run superfast in those conditions. An early break was also unlikely—in a stacked field that included a former world record holder, the course record holder, the Olympic champion, and former winners of Boston and New York, there was simply too much risk in trying to break everyone else from a long way out. All of that helped me, given that I was a couple weeks shy of peak fitness. I went toward the front only when the wind was briefly at our backs or sides, sometimes to slow the pace down, sometimes just to let them know I was there.

For most of my career, the tougher the conditions, the better for me. In retrospect, that year in New York was the last time I placed better in tough conditions than I "should" have, going by entrants' personal bests. I was thirty-nine on race day. My ability to overcome short-term physical adversity was decreasing. You're probably aware of this phenomenon if you've reached a certain age—you experience unusual conditions or an unexpected movement as more of a shock to the system. Two years later, at the Olympic Marathon in Rio, I should have been the one thriving on a day that featured high humidity and slick footing. Instead, as I'll describe in Chapter 24, I seemed to be more affected than others.

There was an upside of my relatively advanced age at the end of my career. I had more experience with and maturity about dealing with tough conditions. Even though my body seemed to be more affected by the conditions, I could counter some of that physical loss with mental strength. One of the best ways to draw on that mental strength is available to everyone, regardless of age: Focus on what you can control, and try not to be brought down by what you can't control.

CONTROLLING WHAT YOU CAN

The Serenity Prayer asks God to grant us the serenity to accept the things we cannot change, the courage to change the things we can, and the wisdom to know the difference. In Chapter 8, I wrote about the importance of knowing what you can and can't control. One of my main points there was that knowing the difference helps you focus your actions. For example, you can't control whether it snows for most of a week when you have a marathon to train for. You can control how you go about running in those conditions, such as by putting grip enhancers on the bottoms of your shoes, or hitting the treadmill, or doing repeated loops of a well-plowed neighborhood.

There are also mental benefits to focusing on what you can control, especially on race day. For example, it's often unseasonably warm and sunny on the day of the Boston Marathon. Many of the people who have trained through harsh winter conditions think, "Ugh, it's going to be hot." That wastes mental energy on thoughts that aren't going to help your race. In contrast, thinking, "Here's what I'm going to do about hydration before and during the marathon" creates the positive thought that you're doing something to improve the situation. (And, of course, it leads to being better prepared physically for the conditions.) Similarly, instead of thinking, "It's going to be windy out there," think, "How can I run to minimize the effects of the wind on my race?" On a day like New York in 2014, that latter approach will mean the obvious physical tactic of running with others for shelter from the wind. There's also the psychological strategy of creating backup goals that I talked about in Chapter 17. Your chances of hitting your primary time goal are lower in tough weather. So what will you do when, only 5 miles into the race, it's obvious the conditions aren't going to allow you to run that fast? With backup goals, you'll find a way to keep pushing.

Race often enough, and you'll also face logistical challenges. Sometimes I was unable to do my full warm-up routine. Maybe the bus to the start ran late and there wasn't enough time to do all of the form drills I usually do. Maybe we had to hand in our bags that would be transported to the finish early, and I didn't have access to the rope I use for stretching. Or maybe they called us to the start line and held us there, and there wasn't space to do my usual 100-meter striders. You've probably experienced being held for several minutes in a cramped corral at your bigger races.

Don't let those challenges defeat you. When I couldn't do pre-race striders I would try to incorporate them into the downhill sections of early miles, or would speed up a little bit approaching the first aid station. With experience, you get better at doing the best you can, whatever the situation.

EVERY PLACE COUNTS

The break finally came after 20 miles. Wilson Kipsang of Kenya, who had set a since-broken marathon world record the previous fall, started pushing. I tried to hang on but was gapped. In training, I had struggled to hit my desired times in the 400-meter repeats I do in the last few weeks of a marathon buildup. That slight loss of turnover is common for veteran runners in their thirties and forties. When Kipsang surged, I wasn't able to change gears quickly enough.

Kipsang soon got the field down to himself, 2013 Boston champ Lelisa Desisa, and 2010 New York winner Gebre Gebremariam, both of Ethiopia. He kept pushing until the end, running 4 of the last 5 miles under 4:40, and then outsprinted Desisa to win in 2:10:59, seven seconds up on Desisa. Thanks to the wind, it was the slowest winning time since 1995.

I was in sixth place after Kipsang's big move. I would have been fine with that placing, given the field, the weather, and my training. But as I've said, "run to win" isn't necessarily about place—it's about knowing you've given it your all. In the last 2 miles the guys ahead of me started to appear closer. There was no reason not to try to catch them.

First I caught the 2012 Olympic and 2013 world champion, Stephen Kiprotich of Uganda. The Mike Cassidy episode from 2013 came to mind. I thought maybe I could talk to Stephen about finishing together; I would have been all over that. But once we were side by side it became obvious he was going to fight for position and the accompanying prize money. We exchanged leads on each other a few times until I pressed ahead. In the final half mile I saw Geoffrey Mutai of Kenya, the Boston and New York course record holder who had won the last two editions of New York. Finishing ahead of someone with his résumé still meant a lot to me. I was able to chase him down and take fourth in 2:13:18.

As I approached the finish line, Gebremariam, who finished third, was making his way back along the course to greet fans. He held out his arm and we slapped hands as I ran past. It was a beautiful symbol of the mutual respect marathoners have for one another. After we finished, Geoffrey complimented me on a great race. "Don't do that again," he said about passing him. We shared a laugh.

Afterward, even my longtime coach Bob Larsen marveled at how, at that point in my career, I still had the inner drive in the final mile to fight for fourth rather than settle for fifth place. My simple answer is that I don't know how else to race. This was a great example of how true competition brings out your best—not because you want to vanquish someone, but because continuing to fight until the end makes you aim higher than you otherwise would. Regardless of the weather conditions, that approach is never outside your control.

2015 BOSTON MARATHON

APRIL 19, 2015

PLACE   **8th**   TIME   **2:12:42**

KEY LESSON

Surprises are always possible, even when you're feeling great. Don't let them keep you from giving your best.

When you run a 5K, you can usually predict your finishing time within a narrow range. Unless you suffer a bad injury or start too fast, you're probably not going to slow significantly in the last mile. You're just not out there long enough to succumb to something like dehydration or muscle cramps.

In a marathon, because you're on the road for so long, all those performance wreckers and more are possible. The need to overcome those challenges adds to the allure of the marathon. Much of what we do in training and on race day lowers the chance of these events. We do long runs and carbo-load so that we don't run out of fuel. We drink throughout the race so that we don't get dehydrated. We do core strength workouts and drills so that we can maintain good running form to the finish.

Still, when you run for hours, your body has plenty of opportunities to present a surprise. I got one such surprise when I tried to defend my Boston Marathon title. As I've said in other chapters, it's on tough days more than good days that our true character is usually revealed.

RETURNING AS CHAMPION

It was such an honor to be feted throughout race week as the defending Boston champion. The outpouring of support was a fresh reminder that my win in 2014 wasn't for me, or even American distance running, but for all of Boston and the running community. That week in particular, anything I said or did was on a bigger scale. There's a responsibility that goes with that, to speak and act in a manner that honorably represents yourself, your family, your sport, your sponsors, and your country.

My pre-race schedule in Boston was intense, with several public appearances each day. Hawi did his usual great job of filtering requests and handling logistics. It's not so much the events themselves that can be tiring but getting to and from each. You've probably experienced this phenomenon with picking up your number at a big race's expo. By the time you go to the venue, navigate the lines, and return to your hotel, several hours may have passed. You think, "I'll just dash in and out," but then you find that much of the day is gone, you're hungry and thirsty, and you've been on your feet a lot longer than you had anticipated.

Some people saw my schedule as evidence that I wasn't seriously committed to defending my title. They don't know me very well if they thought that. I've never taken any success for granted or rested on my laurels. For example, on the Friday night before the race, a huge crowd packed the Old South Church, right by the marathon finish line, for an event celebrating the release of my book *Meb for Mortals*. It featured a panel discussion about my career and effect on American distance running. Rather than draining me, the event got me fired up and more confident for Monday.

I was fitter than I'd been when I won, thanks to no minor injuries and better weather during my altitude training in Mammoth Lakes in the month before the race. I ran faster at the NYC Half Marathon four weeks before than the year before. I got in a 28-miler at a good pace at very high altitude three weeks out. In the right kind of race, there was no reason I couldn't run faster than in 2014.

Of course, I was more focused on place than time. I felt a lot of pressure to repeat as champion. My options for how to do that were limited. I couldn't use the wild card of an early solo break this time. I would have to play my cards very close to the chest. I would respond to moves as warranted, as I had since the beginning of my marathon career, but would otherwise sit tight. I imagined bottling the energy that would be pouring out of Boston's always amazing crowds, and then drawing on that energy over the last 5K to 5 miles to produce something special.

TAKEN BY SURPRISE

It was a little windy, rainy, and cool when we set off from Hopkinton. I reminded myself to stay hydrated and run with my fluid bottles for a long time unless an aid station coincided with a serious move.

The pace was solid from the start. Lelisa Desisa of Ethiopia, the 2013 champion, seemed eager to keep things going at a good clip. Message to me: "You won't be running away from us this year, and we're going to make you work for it." I was fine with the pace. It was a treat and an honor to interact with the crowd. The year before, they had been so boisterous in their contribution to reclaiming the roads after the bombings. This year, their excitement felt more focused on me. Above the din I heard my name called or chants of "USA! USA!" I tried not to get carried away by the early excitement. Like I said, I wanted to bottle that energy and save it for after Heartbreak Hill. I gave an occasional thumbs-up or, through really tight spots, fist bumps. A pack of eleven of us passed halfway in 1:04:00. I gave the crowd a little "USA! USA!" chant like I did on Boylston in 2014.

There were no big moves in the Newton hills. My fellow U.S. Olympian Dathan Ritzenhein seesawed between the back of the pack to leading it, then back to the back. Dathan is a tough, fearless racer who does best with a steady, grinding pace rather than a big kick at the end. He's never afraid to take the pace in the second half of a race if it starts to lag. It was exciting to have two Americans so involved in how the race was playing out at that point of the marathon. I was still doing as little of the work as possible and feeling great as we came up and over Heartbreak Hill for the final five miles. My race plan was playing out perfectly.

With about four miles to go, the day suddenly got harder. The pack was down to seven, and I was the only American in it. I was drinking from my bottle, something I've done hundreds if not thousands of times at race pace, when the fluid wouldn't go down. Suddenly I was coughing and choking. I started to throw up, not from an upset stomach but because of my body wanting to get rid of the fluid in my throat. I had to stop.

We were already moving well at that point. When my incident happened, Desisa and others in the pack noticed and picked up the pace even more. That doubled my challenge—I had to get back to normal breathing, and now I had to run even faster than the leaders to catch back up to them.

Once it started, the problem was with me the rest of the way. I wound up stopping five times in the last four miles. These were brief stops, standing with my hands on my legs trying to throw up. Then I'd resume running as hard as I could, which only worsened the catching feeling in my throat. I pretty quickly accepted I wouldn't be repeating as champion. (Desisa wound up claiming his second title.)

This was one of the most frustrating incidents of any race in my career. It happened not because of a mistake I made in training, or my race plan, or anything else I could later evaluate and improve on. It didn't even make sense in the context of the race. The vomiting I endured at New York in 2011 partly stemmed from the race having been so fast from the start. That wasn't the case here. It was just an unwelcome surprise, something completely out of the blue. Here I was, so highly motivated to give my best, but it just wouldn't be possible to do so that day.

FINISHING IN STYLE

Running in the lead pack for 22 miles, rocking the #1 bib as the defending champion, was incredible. It means a lot to me to be able to say, "I ran the Boston Marathon, then I won the Boston Marathon, then I wore bib #1 at the Boston Marathon."

I knew I wouldn't win. I also knew it was really important to carry on the best I could. I thought about who was ahead of me, and who would be best able to survive the late-race surging and who might be coming back to me. I resolved to fight for every position.

The spectators were a great help that day. Rather than the general roar with occasional personalized cheers that accompanied being in the lead pack, now the support was all focused on me. It was a more intimate connection with the crowd. When I ran past I'd hear variations of "Go, Meb!" and shouts of thanks for my win. When I had to stop to try to vomit, there would first be an eerie silence, then, "C'mon, Meb!" and "You can do it!" and "USA! USA! USA!" and "Thank you for winning last year!" Then there'd be a roar when I started running again. Their support strengthened my determination to finish as well as I could. I wanted to embody the idea that running to win isn't just about finishing first but getting the best out of yourself even when things aren't going the way you'd like them to. People get motivated to do their best in all parts of their lives when they see examples of that.

Whenever I was dropped from the lead pack in a marathon, I fought the rest of the way to reclaim as many spots as I could. Since watching Boston in 2013 from the finish grandstand and finishing with Mike Cassidy in New York that year, however, I also had a newfound appreciation for the symbolism of runners crossing the line together. The following year in New York, when I caught Geoffrey Mutai and Stephen Kiprotich in the final two miles, I thought about asking if they wanted to finish together. But it didn't happen. Once a repeat win was out of the cards in Boston, I thought how special it would be to finish with someone. Doing so would mean a lot to me and (I hoped) the person I finished with, and it would be a great symbol of sportsmanship.

In Boston the elite women start about half an hour before the elite men and the first wave of qualifiers. The first male finishers typically pass some of the women in the final miles. I caught up to one of the women with about 1 kilometer to go and thought about running in with her. But I had passed Tadese Tola of

Ethiopia a few minutes earlier, and my desire to fight for every spot outweighed the appeal of finishing with someone. With the crowd screaming for me every step of the way, I pressed on for the famous final stretch of right on Hereford Street, then left on Boylston to the finish.

I cruised down Boylston, acknowledging the crowd and enjoying the moment. As I approached the finish I looked up ahead and saw another woman. I didn't know who she was; I just saw a blue singlet and thought I'd like to finish with her. I had to sprint to catch her, which I did just a few steps from the line. I said, "Good job, give me your hand, we're going to finish together." She, understandably, was initially startled, but we were able to join hands and raise our arms in time to stride across the finish line together.

The moment became even more memorable when I learned she was Hillary Dionne, a Charlestown, Massachusetts, resident whose blue singlet bore the Boston Athletic Association (BAA) logo. It was like fate—I couldn't have asked for a better person to finish with. The image of last year's champion hand in hand with a local runner cemented the fact that the Boston Marathon was again a beacon of positivity. The race didn't end like I wanted to, but it definitely ended on a high note.

2015 NEW YORK CITY MARATHON

NOVEMBER 1, 2015

PLACE **7th**   TIME **2:13:32**

KEY LESSON

Marathoning and life aren't binary. You can juggle multiple goals and still accomplish a lot.

I f you looked at the fields on the starting line of the 2015 New York City Marathon, you would have seen almost no elite American runners. That's not because the race organizers didn't want them there. The New York Road Runners have long supported and been eager to host top Americans.

Few Americans ran New York that year because the Olympic Marathon Trials, the race that would select the three men and three women who would run the marathon at the 2016 Rio Games, would be held three and a half months later. Many of the top contenders for the Olympic team skipped a fall marathon. They wanted to focus on training and didn't want to risk injury or lingering fatigue come February from racing 26.2 miles in October or November.

So why was I, the oldest of the top Trials contenders, on the line in New York?

RISING TO THE CHALLENGE

The 2016 Olympic Trials would be my last chance to make an Olympic team. I never viewed running New York in 2015 as a barrier to earning one more Olympic berth. Instead, I saw doing the two marathons within fifteen weeks as the sort of challenge I thrive on. I'd pulled off a much tighter New York/ Trials double—only ten weeks between—four years earlier. Aiming to do so as a forty-year-old was the sort of personally meaningful goal that is exciting and daunting enough to bring out my best. For me, the two marathons were complementary, not contradictory.

Most of my competitors chose the opposite approach of a very long buildup to the Trials. My tactic may not be best for all; everyone needs to do what they think works for them. At the same time, I sometimes wondered about people taking this approach. Of course you need to focus on the Olympic Trials and do as many things right as possible in the months before. But that doesn't mean professional runners can't race! I'm not the only elite runner who has run two high-quality marathons in a relatively short time. A number of recent Boston Marathon winners have raced well at the Dubai Marathon three months earlier. I'm not saying they or you should run several marathons a year and expect to do well in all of them. But if it suits your psyche, it's possible to run a decent number of marathons and use one as a bridge to the next. (For pros, the financial aspect of the fall marathon never hurts. Sometimes it's a business decision and being realistic with your God-given talent to compete and recover.)

More importantly, your status on a given day six months away is never guaranteed. You could grind away at your training week after week after week and get injured or overly fatigued. You might catch a cold the week of the race. As I learned in 2006, you could be felled by food poisoning or something else with just days to go. You might even fall during the race or get a cramp or suffer any number of in-the-moment issues that dash that dream.

Life is a balancing act. The more eggs you put in one basket, the bigger the loss if something happens to that basket. Movies and other forms of entertainment often idealize the person who has one big dream and spends a lifetime ignoring anything that doesn't help her achieve it. I love those stories. I've talked a lot in this book about how much winning New York and Boston drove me for years. There were many sacrifices needed to reach those goals. I still had a life, though. I accomplished other things in running, I broke new ground in running sponsorship, I was a devoted husband and father. One running goal doesn't have to preclude others, nor does it have to preclude being successful and ambitious in other parts of your life. Even back in high school I understood this balance. As a senior I skipped a big cross-country meet to take the SATs. Doing well on the SATs gave me more college options, which in turn helped my running. One step can have many payoffs.

Another thing: Although most people can't run a marathon every week, you do need to give yourself a chance to succeed. One reason I'm the only marathoner in history with Boston and New York titles and an Olympic medal is that I repeatedly put myself in a position for those great things to happen. Most retired athletes I've talked with say they wish they'd stuck around a little longer and aimed for one more big race. That wasn't the case with me! I finished my career feeling I'd done one or two too many marathons. But I have no regrets about that. As in any one marathon, I'd rather have finished feeling like I was tapped out than that I hadn't given it everything I had. That includes all the altitude training, mileage, and daily sacrifices that went into racing my best. Racing is the frosting on the cake of months of training.

All of that was behind my eagerness to do the New York/Olympic Trials double again. Also, in 2015 I still thought that on a great day I could win again. It's important to be open to great things happening, and seizing those opportunities when they arise.

This time, I had an additional goal. New York would be my first marathon since turning forty the previous May. I had already broken the American masters (age forty and over) records at 15K, 10 miles, 20K, and the half marathon. The marathon mark of 2:13:57 was well within my capability—I'd run faster on the New York course just one year earlier. I was heading to New York to compete with the best, not to go out at the slower pace needed to break the masters record and exert myself as little as possible before the Trials. Getting under 2:13:57, however, was in the back of my mind. Breaking the masters record was a backup goal.

JUGGLING AT RACE PACE

This was the year that Spike Lee was the grand marshal at New York. He rode near those of us in the lead pack for much of the race and was easy to spot with his bright orange sunglasses. I kept giving him the thumbs-up sign. I wasn't pandering or hamming it up. My training had gone well, with a couple 27-milers and some good tempo runs between 13 and 15 miles. I was ready to be competitive, to get on the podium on a good day, and to win on a perfect day.

I was optimistic once the race was under way. The field was absolutely stacked: defending champion Wilson Kipsang of Kenya; his countryman Geoffrey Kamworor, the world half marathon and cross-country champion; Lelisa Desisa and Yemane Tsegay of Ethiopia, who had finished first and second in Boston that spring; and Stanley Biwott of Kenya, who had become the latest member of the exclusive sub-2:04 marathon club that April in London. As usually occurs in New York, though, none of the guys with the turbocharged personal bests were eager to run hard from the start. The early miles were moderate, at around 2:11 marathon pace, and then got even slower. Thirteen of us passed halfway in 1:06:49—barely fast enough to get under the U.S. masters record that was one of my backup goals! I wasn't worried, because with all the talent and speed in the pack, I knew that at some point we would start running much faster. I figured that point would be the usual spot, the slightly downhill, crowd-crazy stretch from mile 17 to mile 19 on First Avenue in Manhattan.

It didn't happen—nobody surged hard while on the fastest part of the course. When there wasn't a big move on First Avenue, I told myself an even bigger push was coming. I thought it would be in the last 5K. I was telling myself, "Stay calm, stay comfortable." I was still running within myself. It was going to be an exciting finish. I just needed to get to the last three miles in Central Park feeling good and under control. After that, I figured, it would get really intense, with the rolling topography of the park contributing to when the moves would be made. I felt I could handle a few superfast miles at that point in the race. I still thought a win was possible.

Unfortunately, they threw a curve: The sub-4:30 miles started with 10K to go. Kamworor was the aggressor. I covered the move. After 90 seconds, my body and mind were stressed to the max. I realized they weren't backing down—there were too many good guys pushing to let up now. I knew that I could run with them for the next mile or two, but then I would have been over-extended with too far to go, and nothing really to show for it. I would be the one being caught by others, I might jeopardize the masters record and, because of struggling in after being broken, I might not be my best at the Trials. I quickly made a conscious decision to back off. I figured some of those who tried to go longer with the break would fall apart and come back to me. I wanted to be the one who gauged his effort properly all the way to the finish.

Up ahead of me, others were suffering from the surging, and for good reason: Kamworor's push had resulted in a 4:24 21st mile. Of the four who made it together to that point, Kip-sang cracked first, followed by Desisa. Biwott took over after a 4:33 23rd mile. He broke Kamworor in Central Park by cover-ing the 5K stretch from 35K (21.7 miles) to 40K (just shy of 25 miles) in an unprecedented 14:19. Biwott's winning time was a modest 2:10:34. The real racing occurred only after 20 miles. When I heard these splits after the race, I was satisfied with the on-the-spot decision I'd made to not try to keep up.

The rest of my race was a microcosm of my larger approach to that year's New York—you can successfully do more than one thing at once. I juggled protecting my position, trying to catch others, and keeping an eye on the clock for the masters record with trying to avoid any late-race move that would prolong my recovery before the Trials. Yuki Kawauchi of Japan and I were neck and neck the final miles. Yuki, the surprise winner of the 2018 Boston Marathon, is an extreme example of not pegging all your work to one do-or-die event. He's run more sub-2:20 marathons than anyone in history and races about twenty times a year against top competition. He even ran a 2:12 marathon two weeks before winning Boston. Yet he's able to give his all every time and appears no worse for the wear.

He certainly wasn't going through the motions that day in New York. Every time I thought I'd broken him, Yuki would fight his way back. I kicked one last time as we reentered Central Park with about 600 meters to go. I wasn't able to drop him, and when he went hard again in the last 400 meters, he gapped me. With the deceptively tough uphill in the final stretch of New York, I was worried that an all-out sprint against Yuki would strain my hamstring. I couldn't take that risk with the Olympic Trials three months away. I finished seventh in 2:13:32, three seconds behind Yuki. The time was comfortably under the U.S. masters record and good enough to make me the top American finisher.

People may have looked at the results and thought that after running 2:13, I'd get right back into training for the Trials. They wouldn't have thought that if they'd seen the ball of my left foot. As almost always happened, the old wound from 2007 was a mess. Priority number one after that year's New York was to make sure it didn't get infected like it did in 2011 so soon before the 2012 Trials.

Even though I wasn't running, I wanted to keep the muscles loose to smooth my eventual return to training. I did a lot of stretching (and sleeping) and got frequent massages. Once my foot felt okay with normal weight bearing, I did a lot of ElliptiGO rides to help maintain my fitness. I resumed light running three weeks after New York, with the Trials less than twelve weeks away. Mentally, I was all set—I had just finished only 47 seconds behind Kipsang, a former world record holder. That evening Kipsang told me, "You looked good throughout the race. You got the Trials." Rather than hurt me, my race in New York increased my confidence that I could be among the top three at the Trials and make my fourth Olympic team.

KEY LESSON

Age is just a number if you learn to listen to your body and adapt to its changing needs.

Immediately after the 2015 New York City Marathon I turned my sights to making my fourth Olympic team. The Trials race in Los Angeles was run a little more than three months after New York. I knew from previous quick turnarounds what I needed to do—recover well, don't rush things, just bring the fitness back.

Although it had been less than two years since I won Boston, some people didn't think I was a top pick for one of the three Olympic spots. I was forty years old on race day and was one of the few top seeds in the race to have run a fall marathon. I reminded myself that age is just a number. So much of the marathon—and life—is a mental game. If you tell yourself, "Oh, I'm forty, my body aches more than it used to, I can't do this, I can't do that," then those limitations you place on yourself can become self-defeating. You start trying not as hard, and then you don't achieve what you're really capable of.

When I say age is just a number, I don't mean you can ignore it. Of course your body is going to change as you age. Starting in my midthirties I began to notice I didn't have as much lean muscle mass as I had in my twenties. Recovery after long runs and hard workouts began to take longer. I struggled to hit the times in short, fast workouts, such as 400-meter repeats, that I had hit ten years earlier.

I was able to keep my career going at that point by listening to rather than fighting my body. I knew I needed to make some changes in my approach to account for the effects of aging. That's not giving in, that's being smart.

One big change I made was being more careful about my diet. I eliminated added sugar and moved away from meals that were overwhelmingly carbohydrate-based. I emphasized more lean protein with every meal to help with muscle recovery. I reduced the portions of most meals and, in contrast to my twenties, when I was a member in good standing of the Clean Plate Club, became familiar with the concept of leftovers. This diet helped me recover from hard training while being at a good weight on marathon race day.

Another big change I made was to switch my training from a seven-day cycle to a nine-day cycle. This change allowed me the extra recovery time I needed so that the runs that really matter—long runs, tempo runs, and interval workouts—made me fitter rather than wore me out. Instead of trying to cram in all my key workouts every week, I took two days of easy to moderate mileage after every long run, tempo run, or interval workout. I was still doing the work but spreading it out so that I could get to the start line healthy.

Finally, I made some mental adjustments to account for the

physical changes. I'm a numbers guy who has records of all his training. If I want to, after doing a tempo run on a course I've run many, many times, I can compare that day's result to what I ran a decade before. I learned that doing so is interesting but not helpful. What's better is a constant dialogue with yourself: How did I feel? Did I put in a good effort without going all out? Are my goals still reasonable?

That mental adjustment is key to so much more than how fast you are in races. It gets back to not getting caught in the negative cycle I mentioned earlier of thinking, "I can't do this thing or that thing as well as I used to, I'm getting old, I should leave ambition to the young." So much of successful aging—in running and life—is acknowledging what has changed while not letting those changes define you. The way you go about achieving your goals will likely change, but the value of pursuing them doesn't have to. Know yourself and keep coming back to this question: Are my goals still reasonable?

Going into the 2016 Trials, the answer to the last question was yes. I had enough experience to know that the training I was doing was good enough physical preparation. On race day, I knew I had a better storehouse of competitive experiences to draw on than anyone else in the field.

LIKING MY ODDS

As I thought about my race plan, I kept telling myself I'd won the world's most prestigious marathon over a top field less than two years ago. And at the Trials, all I had to do to meet my goal was finish in the top three. Did I go in settling for third place? Absolutely not. When the gun went off I went for the win. But I thought that even on a day I don't have my A game, I should be able to make the Olympic team. I'd done the work, and after twenty-two marathons I had enough experience to know what that training meant in terms of my readiness. Unlike a lot of the younger guys in the field, I wasn't thinking, "Sure, I did the training, but how will I feel on race day?"

Over the years there have been enough surprises at the Olympic Marathon Trials that you don't want to discount anybody. But realistically I figured there were five or six guys to watch in the race. (My good friend and longtime rival Abdi Abdirahman would have been one of them, but he had to withdraw before the race with an injury.) There were young up-and-comers like Tyler Pennel and Jared Ward, who had won the last two national marathon titles, and Luke Puskedra, who had the fastest American time in the marathon in 2015. There was fellow Olympic Marathon veteran Dathan Ritzenhein. And there was the wild card of Galen Rupp, the 2012 Olympic silver medalist at 10,000 meters, who was making his marathon debut at the Trials. I knew he would be tough and that he had a realistic shot at winning. But he was going to have to earn it if I had anything to say about it.

The temperature was in the 70s for most of the race, with a bright sun beating down on us on an exposed course. The heat was noticeable almost immediately. I figured that would mean a cautious early pace. I reminded myself what I wanted to accomplish—to earn one last chance to wear the USA jersey and to give my girls the memory of a lifetime.

With the race taking place in the city where I'd gone to college, the course was lined with old friends and fans. Skechers had made me a special uniform and shoes for the day featuring the yellow and blue of UCLA. Despite having lived in California since I came to the United States, this was my first marathon in the state. It felt like a graduation and homecoming combined.

I reminded myself to not get emotional early on. My plan: Be patient, let the field unwind itself, hammer the last 10K to separate the top three, and then go for the win. The main scenario I wanted to avoid was being in a pack of five or six with a mile to go against younger guys who might be able to outsprint me. I figured that if I followed this plan and had an average day, I could make the team. My mind was at peace.

MAKING THE TEAM

Fifteen of us went through halfway on 2:13 marathon pace. This was the conservative opening I had counted on. Watch for moves from the right people, I told myself, and be ready to make the move yourself if necessary.

It wasn't necessary. After 15 miles, Tyler Pennel dramatically increased the pace. We had been running most miles at around 5:05 to 5:10. Tyler moved to the front and ran the 16th mile in 4:56, and then the 17th mile in 4:52. When Tyler passed the 17-mile mark, he had only two companions—Galen Rupp and me.

Tyler had been on a tear in shorter races in the months before the Trials, including a 3:58 mile on the track. He was one of the young, fast guys I didn't want to have to contend with as part of a big group late in the race. So it worked out well that, with 9 miles to go, there were only three of us in the lead pack. I told Tyler, "We're good, we're good," meaning that we'd accomplished the first big goal of getting the group down to three, the magic number for making the team. Usually in these situations the thing to do is to relax a little bit once the break is made, and then resume the real racing closer to the finish to determine first, second, and third places. I knew that Galen, in his first marathon and with his track background of sprinting at the end of races, would wait to set out on his own.

But Tyler wasn't content to have broken almost all of the rest of the field. He was running for the win, from a long way out.

He kept pushing—miles 18 and 19 were 4:52 and 4:56. Tyler was the one who made this race what it was, and I respect his courage, but I think he made a mistake in running like this. In the Trials, third is as good as first, because you're going to be named an Olympian forever. At this point in the race, his goal should have been to clearly separate three of us from the rest of the field, not go for the kill. That was especially true against Galen and me, with both of us having Olympic silver medals and having set the American record for 10K.

Despite Tyler's continued push, I didn't panic. My experience told me it was unlikely that Tyler would keep running 2:07 marathon pace until the finish. Sure enough, in the 20th mile I sensed that he was starting to falter. I pushed to capitalize on his weakness. Galen went with me, and by the time we reached the 20-mile mark we had gapped Tyler by five seconds. Tyler eventually faded to fifth.

Things got a little weird once it was just Galen and me. Despite the wide-open roads we were on, Galen ran like you do on the track, staying as close as possible to your competitors. When I say as close as possible, in this case I mean it literally—he bumped into me a few times. Once is okay, especially if afterward you acknowledge your mistake, maybe offer a handshake or a "my bad." But three times, with no acknowledgment? Then we have a problem. I said a few choice words and pointed to the ground to remind him we had the whole road to ourselves.

Galen pushed hard in the 23rd mile, running a 4:47 mile that I was unable to match. I reminded myself that "run to win" means different things in different contexts. Here, winning meant making my fourth Olympic team at age forty. Over-extending myself to try to cover Galen's surge could have jeopardized that main goal, because I might have hit the Wall in the last couple of miles and fallen to fourth place.

Although the outcome of any marathon isn't sure until you cross the finish line, I was pretty psyched those last couple of miles in Los Angeles. I was running within myself and knew I was going to place second. Adding to the excitement was seeing a lot of familiar faces in the closing stretches: friends, former teammates and classmates, my parents, my brothers and sisters, and even my ninth-grade English teacher were on the sidelines cheering for me. Of course it's a huge accomplishment to qualify for the Olympics. For it to happen in the city where my running really took off made the moment that much more special. I started celebrating over the last half mile, pumping my fist, pointing to people in the crowd, grabbing an American flag for the run to the finish.

Galen won in 2:11:12. Jared Ward, already a master of pacing in only his fourth marathon, moved into third place in the 21st and finished in that position in 2:13:00 to complete our team. I was very satisfied knowing I'd beat all but one guy in the country, despite being more than a decade older than most of them. I had used my experience and collected wisdom in my preparation and on race day to get the best out of myself. And speaking of age, a bonus: My time of 2:12:20 broke my own U.S. masters marathon record.

Having Yordanos and our girls at the finish was a memory I'll always cherish. I started thinking about our next family running trip, to Rio de Janeiro for the 2016 Olympics. On race day, I would be forty-one, the oldest U.S. Olympic marathoner in history. In the weeks after, I heard from a lot of people my age or older how inspired they were by my run. Some said they were now less likely to let their age limit them, and that they were rethinking how ambitious to be in running or work or other parts of life. I took these messages to heart as I started preparing for Rio. I was eager to show the world that age is just a number.

2016 OLYMPIC MARATHON
(Rio de Janeiro, Brazil)

AUGUST 21, 2016

PLACE **33rd**   TIME   **2:16:46**

KEY LESSON

Finish what you start and make the most of it.

The marathon in Rio would be my last Olympics. You might think that with it being my fourth Games I'd be a bit blasé about the whole thing. If anything, I was the opposite. At previous Olympics, I had been all business before my races. With two of those races being the marathon, which traditionally closes out the Games, I arrived on the scene just days before. No opening ceremony, no attending other competitions, certainly no partying with international athletes.

This time would be different (well, except for the partying). Our daughters were now old enough to really enjoy and remember their time at such a special event. Yordanos and I wanted to make it a family trip with all the trappings—go to the opening ceremony, watch competitions at venues, and be tourists in the many days on site before the marathon. I joked with Yordanos that I was going to gain 50 pounds and show up on the starting line looking like a black Stay Puft Marshmallow Man next to the world's top marathoners. Think of the photo opportunities!

Of course, the competitor in me overruled that. It being my final Olympics meant that I should do my best to be at my best. Because of concerns over the Zika virus, we wound up traveling to Rio only five days before the marathon. I spent that time relaxing at my hotel and getting insights on the course from the American female marathoners, who had raced the previous week. When I toed the line in Rio, I was at my usual racing weight of 121.

RACING IN THE RAIN

Eliud Kipchoge of Kenya was the overwhelming favorite. He'd been the dominant marathoner in the world the previous few years and never had a bad race. He could run faster than anyone in the field, and with a résumé that included Olympic and world championship medals on the track, he wasn't going to be foiled by a tactical race. I knew I couldn't compete with Kipchoge if he showed up with his A game.

I thought I had a chance against the rest of the field. My training went well, with no hiccups. The experience that came with being the oldest in the field would come in handy; I'd already been in marathons with one of the many ways the race could play out. I thought that if everything went well and I got a few breaks, I could fight for the bronze medal. As I had in Athens twelve years earlier, I packed my medal ceremony jacket with my post-race gear.

Race day was wet, with rain before and occasionally during the marathon, and very high humidity. As in my first Olympic marathon in 2004, I ran more toward the back than the front in the early miles. In a field of about 150, rather than several thousand, there was no risk of getting caught behind a crowd and missing moves. Around the 10K mark I worked my way up to the middle of the lead group. It was fun and extremely exciting to once again be in the mix among the who's who of world marathoning. I was running within myself. *Caution* was the watchword on a course full of potholes, puddles, and sharp 180-degree turns.

People were keying off Kipchoge, who at one point told others not to worry, he wasn't making his move yet, when he sped up to get a clear shot at his bottle at an aid station. He and I talked a bit, with him telling me, "Good job, keep it up." I also talked with and ran beside my teammate Jared Ward. We encouraged and helped each other to stay relaxed and watchful in the huge pack. More than forty of us passed halfway in 1:05:50, a pace I felt I could hold to the end. I told myself the race was playing into my hands, that my experience was going to pay off, that I just needed to be patient and ready for the inevitable moves.

FIGHT TO THE FINISH

Just two tenths of a mile later, everything went south.

I was running to Jared's left when I felt a sudden urge to vomit. I said to him, "Let me out, let me out." He thought I meant I wanted space to run a little more freely and said, "No, you're good, you have room, stay where you are." I said, "No, you have no idea. I need to get out, it's urgent. Otherwise I'm going to throw up on someone right here." That got his attention! Jared gave me room to sprint to the side of the road. I put my hands on my thighs and tried to throw up.

This incident was different from what had ailed me at New York in 2011 or Boston in 2015. In New York, my stomach was upset from the very fast pace. The harder you run, the more that blood is diverted from other body parts to your working muscles. One result is that your digestion slows and you become more likely to vomit. In Boston, the problem was that some drink went down the wrong way. I kept trying to vomit but couldn't. In Rio, I eventually decided, I was felled by a side effect of heat hives. As I said in Chapter 22, toward the end of my career I went from being someone who thrived in tough race conditions to someone who seemed more affected by them than my competitors. In my buildup for Rio, I'd done some noon runs in extra clothing and had sat in a sauna for up to thirty minutes, to prepare for racing in the heat. The dry mountain air of Mammoth Lakes or the sauna, it turned out, didn't help me with race day's high humidity.

Counting the stop, my 14th mile was 5:21, about 20 seconds slower than when I was with the lead pack. I could still see that pack. I told myself not to panic, that I would be able to catch back up. Their pace remained moderate, so it would be better in terms of energy efficiency to try to rejoin them gradually than launch a big push to catch them quickly.

I collected myself and ran the 15th mile in 5:08, then the 16th in 5:04. I thought about my race at the London Games four years earlier, where I went from almost dropping out to finishing fourth. I told myself I was going to rejoin the group and then would still be in position to fight for a medal.

Instead, I had to stop again. My 17th mile was another 5:21, just as the leaders were starting to ratchet down the pace. I told myself a top-ten finish was still possible. But then I had to stop again, and again, and again. Each time I tried to vomit but nothing came out. Finishing in the top ten wasn't going to happen. I thought, "Just get to the finish, whatever it takes."

I wound up stopping almost every mile the rest of the race. Even though finishing thirty-third wasn't close to the result I wanted, the last 10 miles were a great experience. Runners from

Peru, Ecuador, South Africa, and elsewhere encouraged me when they ran by during one of my stops. "Come on, Meb," or, "Good job, keep it going," they'd say, sometimes while moving to the side of the road to tap me on the shoulder. To have the respect of my fellow marathoners from around the world made a trying situation so much better. It felt like my peers were treating me to a global victory lap near the end of my career. I'll cherish that experience for the rest of my life.

PRIDE AFTER A FALL

I'm a great fan of Joan Benoit, who wore a hat and waved it to the crowd when she won the first women's Olympic Marathon in 1984. I'd worn a hat during the Trials in February, but, to Joan's disappointment, I didn't tip it at the end, because I was so in the moment and excited about making the team. I also wore one in Rio because of the rain. As I (finally) ran down the long straightaway to the finish, I checked around me—I wasn't going to catch the guy ahead of me, and there was a decent gap to the guy behind me. I thought, "It's my last Olympics, I didn't have the race I wanted, but I'm going to finish with my head held high and wave my hat to the crowd, in honor of Joanie."

I still get a laugh out of what happened next. I reached to take off my hat just before the finish, and my left leg slipped on the slick surface. Suddenly, boom, I went down on my knee, and then was sprawled on the road. I'd always wanted to do a gymnast's split, but not like that.

The finish area at Carnival Stadium went dead quiet. (When I watched the incident later, it looked much worse than it felt.) I looked up and could see the finish line right at my head, but I hadn't crossed it yet. I dragged myself to the finish, with my chest on the line. I thought, "I have to let them know I'm okay, so I guess I'm going to do push-ups." I did three, one for each daughter, and the crowd went crazy with cheering.

That moment had more resonance than if I'd finished eleventh running hard the whole way in. "Meb push-ups" immediately became a thing, with clips of my slip and recovery going viral on social media. I joked about it later when I found Jared, who had placed sixth with a PR behind Kipchoge's winning time of 2:08:44. In the days and weeks after, I heard from other runners who have fallen while running. They congratulated me on quickly converting a scary, embarrassing moment into a victory. Many runners, including some of my fellow Olympians, posted video of themselves doing push-ups to show their appreciation for how I'd handled the situation.

We've all fallen, literally and figuratively. What matters is what you do once you're down. My race in Rio was a fall of sorts, being so far off what I'd hoped for and felt capable of. By persevering and committing to finish, I was rewarded with expressions of respect from my competitors, and I set what I hope is an example for my girls.

The same goes for the actual fall at the finish. I was once running along Lake Michigan in Chicago when I saw a man running toward me fall. He got up, resumed running toward me, and then when we were close to each other, he dropped and did push-ups. He got back up, said, "In your honor," and resumed running. I didn't win a medal in Rio, but I may have found an even better way to inspire others. Now I see lots of people doing a push-up at the finish of a half marathon or marathon. I love it. It's not how many times you fall, but how many times you get back up. You never know who's watching and who will be inspired.

2017 BOSTON MARATHON

APRIL 17, 2017

PLACE **13th**   TIME   **2:17:00**

KEY LESSON

Running—and life—is never a solo project.

B y now you've probably noticed I'm not one to rest on his laurels. When I ran New York seventy days after winning the silver medal at the 2004 Olympics, I was all in for the win. After I won Boston, I got myself into even better shape for the next year's race to try to repeat as champion. I love accomplishing one thing and almost immediately looking ahead to the next challenge.

Probably the only time I didn't feel like that was after the 2017 Boston Marathon. The penultimate marathon of my career was such a struggle, such a grind, that afterward I dreaded the thought of running New York that fall. Only when I was further removed from the fatigue and dissatisfaction of Boston could I appreciate the experience and what it said about how special the running community is. I knew they would help finish my career on a high note, no matter the result.

But I'm getting ahead of myself.

THE LONGEST MILE(S)

My twenty-fifth marathon was much like the 25th mile of most marathons. It was unrelentingly difficult, and it seemed to go on forever. The fact that the finish was near somehow made it harder, not easier, to get through: How could it be taking so long?! And how could I then find the strength for one more (mile or marathon)?

I had a much more positive mind-set on the starting line. My training hadn't been great, but it was solid. I felt capable of running 2:12 on the course in the warm, sunny conditions. In the right sort of race, I thought I could place in the top three. My backup goal of finishing in the top ten was very realistic.

For me, the first few miles of a marathon usually gave a sense of how my legs would feel throughout the race. Things were fine, clicking right along, as a large pack of us ran through Ashland, Framingham, and other early checkpoints. I felt comfortable and confident as we cruised through the 10-mile mark in Natick and made our way toward the scream tunnel at Wellesley College and the halfway mark.

That all changed just past the 12-mile mark. There was a push from the front of the pack up a little hill. With the group twenty strong, I needed to cover the move to meet my place goals. I went to pick up the pace and . . . it didn't work. I wasn't sore or tight. There was just no response from my legs when my mind said, "Pick it up to stay with the pack." My usual quick turnover and pop off the ground had been replaced by the feeling of running in jelly.

To this day I don't have an explanation. For the first time in a marathon, my quads were simply dead—with 14 miles to go! The move from the front wasn't a huge one, just the sort that happens at that point in the race as some want to start whittling the pack. It's the kind that you cover because you have to and because you know it won't last all that long. That type of tactical racing was my forte throughout my career, like when I whittled the pack in New York in 2005 by running 8:57 between miles 16 and 18. So when, out of nowhere, I couldn't cover such a move only 12 miles into the marathon, I freaked out. I wondered what was going on my with body. As if watching from the outside, I saw the pack pulling away and me being unable to do anything about it. I felt defeated.

CARRIED BY THE CROWD

The marathon is always a long way. But if you have a bigger problem, especially before halfway, it becomes an ultramarathon. (By the way, I often get asked if I have interest in running ultras, or races longer than 26.2 miles. I feel like I already did in some of my marathons! Going farther than that is not for me.)

Boston 2017 was the ultimate case of this reality for me. I tell people that if you're properly trained, the first 18 miles should be comfortable and under control. Never had I reached halfway knowing things would only get more difficult. Even at the 2012 Olympics, where I almost dropped out, I could convince myself that I was in a bad patch that might pass if I persevered. Here, I knew the "bad patch" would last the remaining several miles to the finish. It was like an extended version of the last 10K of my first marathon—brutal and draining, with my physical duress made worse by being unable to rally psychologically.

My one ace in the hole: the crowds along the course. The route was absolutely jammed with fans on a great day for spectating. They were aware that this was my last Boston as an elite runner and were more enthusiastic than ever in their cheering for me. Early on, when I was with the lead pack, I could occasionally hear my name shouted out above the general roar. To be honest, I sometimes felt bad for the runners around me. Here, as at many races, people were yelling my name but not those of my competitors. There were times in my career when a competitor jokingly told me, "They can read my name, too."

Now that I was running the final 14 miles solo, the cheering was far more personal—things like "Go, Meb!" or "Great job, Meb!" or "Go get 'em, Meb!" ("I would if I could," I thought when I heard the last one.) Some could tell I was struggling and would encourage me to keep going or stay on it. Others seemed to sense my internal monologue and yelled, "C'mon, Meb, you can do it!"

The crowd was in my corner the whole rest of the race, through the Newton hills, up and over Heartbreak Hill, by Boston College, and, most raucously, as I finally made my way down Boylston Street to the finish. I was able to compose myself in that final stretch and acknowledge the crowd as I finished thirteenth in 2:17:00. I considered the fans there stand-ins for all those along the route who had helped me get to the finish, not just on that day but every mile of the five times I raced Boston. Together we produced something magical.

THE UNLONELINESS OF THE LONG-DISTANCE RUNNER

That day in Boston symbolized the team approach to running that was true throughout my career.

Most people think of runners as self-reliant, solo athletes. That's only partially true. Sure, we're self-driven—you don't train for and run marathons without a lot of inner drive. As I said in Chapter 12, the most important part of a good goal is that it be personally meaningful. Almost everyone on the starting line of a marathon has that box checked.

But almost everyone on the starting line of a marathon is also there with the support of many others. You might see someone running down the street early in the morning and applaud her commitment. What you don't see are the friends and family who probably help her, in ways small and large, be a runner. Maybe it's the spouse who takes on more housework while she's marathon training, or the neighbor who watches her kids so she can get in a long run, or the friend on the other side of the country who sends supportive texts on tough days. Her marathon itself is also a community event, held up by the hard work of race organizers, volunteers, and spectators.

In my case, I was helped by so many people throughout my career. Coach Larsen never stopped believing in me or showing up for me. He, Mario Arce, Dirk Addis, Rich Levy, Jim Tabb, Sara Chavez, and others were literally there for me, as bike pacers during tempo runs and long runs. Suresh Chaurushiya, Gary Ochman, and others took me into their homes during training stints. My brother Hawi took care of my business affairs so that I could concentrate on training. Hawi even managed my daily schedule for me when things got really crazy.

And of course my biggest supporter has been Yordanos. She is the backbone of our family and has always been very generous with her time to help me become the person of my dreams. She is a great mom to our children, handles the family finances, and otherwise works behind the scenes to make sure things run smoothly. Her support allowed me the time and liberty to do what was necessary not only in training but also in my role as a running ambassador. She's usually not there to hear or see when I have the opportunity to inspire others, or grieve with people who lost their loved ones to cancer or other challenges, or celebrate their magical moments of losing weight and attempting their first marathon. She has faith that the sacrifices she makes on my behalf help not only me but countless others.

This teamwork idea is a great example of how marathoning is a metaphor for life. We're ultimately responsible for our results, on the race course and elsewhere, but we owe so much to others for their support in allowing us to do what we do. And, as with the thousands who urged me along to Boylston Street that day in Boston, we're all buoyed by the kindness of strangers.

In turn, we all only reach our personal best—as runners and people—by giving back to others. I like to help other runners because I know how much harder it is for many people than it is for me. I think back to what school was like for me as a reminder that we all have different talents. I was the one plugging away, writing five or six versions of a ten-page paper, because that was what it took to get it right. I had classmates who could crank out the same paper in a day and get an A to my B minus.

Not that I didn't work hard during my marathon career. Boy, did I work hard. Still, I know that running comes more naturally to me than it does to many people. I want to help them in the same way that others helped me in school, or that the crowds helped me in Boston. Whether they finish a marathon in three hours or five hours or seven hours, they have my respect. All runners know how hard our sport is and that we need each other's help and encouragement. That knowledge lies behind the examples of camaraderie among competitors I've described in many chapters.

So even though my result in my final Boston was far from what I wanted, I happily accepted the congratulations of fans and fellow runners afterward. They knew I had given my best on a difficult day. It was now time to recover, then lean on my team as I ran to win one more time in New York.

KEY LESSON

Whether you're having a good or a bad day, get to the finish line as best you can.

After my first marathon, a trip to my native land of Eritrea motivated me to give the distance another shot. Before my last marathon, a trip back to Eritrea motivated me yet again to give the distance my best shot one more time.

I'll admit that during and after my twenty-fifth marathon, in Boston that spring, I thought, "I signed up for one marathon too many." I considered running number 26 in New York as a 26.2-mile easy celebration. Then my better instincts took over. My final competitive marathon was the equivalent of the last mile of a marathon. The most appropriate way to cap my career was to do what I always had—run to win. Giving your best over the whole course is what life is about. Doing so in the marathon is a microcosm of that model of excellence.

I resolved that when I crossed that finish line in New York in 2017, I could say I gave my all, just as I did when I crossed the same finish line fifteen years earlier in my first marathon.

WITH A LITTLE HELP FROM MY FRIENDS

Yordanos and I decided to take the girls to Eritrea for much of the summer. We had relatives to visit on both sides of the family, and we wanted our daughters to learn more about their roots. Family took priority during our two months there. My running was more maintenance mileage than serious marathon training—many days I'd squeeze in six or seven miles early in the morning before a full day of family visits. My main goal was to come home in late August without injury or sickness so that I could start my marathon buildup in earnest.

Eritrea has a strong and growing elite running scene. The greatest half marathon runner in history, Zersenay Tadese, is Eritrean, as is Ghirmay Ghebreslassie, the 2015 world marathon champion who would be defending his New York title that fall. I was honored to be asked to join a large group of aspiring elites for a few of their workouts. I'm not going to lie—I struggled to keep up with them on their hard sessions. I hadn't done interval workouts since before Boston. I was huffing and puffing, especially at the 7,000-plus feet of altitude, while most of the group of twenty-five were ahead of me. Still, I enjoyed the camaraderie and wished I'd trained in a group more in my career. Sharing the workload and the respect for discipline made the workout go by fast.

As humbling as these workouts were, they and the entire trip to Eritrea were a blessing in disguise in regard to my final marathon. Almost none of the guys I ran with there had ever raced outside the country. Their dream is to get noticed by someone—an agent, a coach, a star runner—who will give them the chance to compete against the rest of the world. They show up every day and work extraordinarily hard in the hope that their dream will come true, even though the odds are against most of them. Spending time with them was a reality check. I told myself to appreciate, not take for granted, my opportunity to live their dream. I returned home from Eritrea rejuvenated and committed to making one more all-in push for New York.

The key part of that push was a final altitude stint in Mammoth Lakes. Being away from my family for five weeks was as difficult as ever, but I kept reminding myself it was a sign of how dedicated I was. I had several consecutive weeks over 100 miles, with a high of 131, only five fewer than my lifetime high. My longest run was 27.7 miles. I had once done a 28-miler on the same course, but as an older and wiser (and okay, more tired) forty-two-year-old, I thought, "27.7 is good enough for today."

Of course, I could also compare my times on intervals and tempo runs to what I'd done in Mammoth Lakes before other marathons. By the end of my stay I was near what I'd been running in 2012 and 2014. The important thing was to get in consistent good efforts rather than think, "It's my last buildup—swing for the fences in every workout." Trying to "win" workouts would have gotten in the way of the main goal of any marathon training block, which is to get to the start line healthy and eager to race. I got a massage every two to three days and did a lot of stretching to help meet that goal. My reward was no bodily issues that compromised my training.

There were times where I sort of watched myself go about my last marathon buildup. I would think, "This is my last run at Lake Mary, at 9,000 feet" or "I just did my last tempo run." As always, I got down to my low-120s racing weight, in part by cutting out refined sugar and watching my portion sizes. It was interesting to think I would never be at that weight again. It was easy to find that discipline. Doing so was like getting to the last mile of a marathon, when you know the finish will come soon, and you can then start the next chapter in your life.

A PRE-RACE CELEBRATION

Preparation will always be the key to success. My mileage, tempo runs, self-care, and so on would be the determinants of how my final marathon went.

I kept this in mind during the hectic week before the marathon. I had thirty-three appearances, press conferences, media interviews, and other events between when I landed in New York and the night before the race. I would leave my hotel room at 6:30 a.m. and get back after 10 p.m. Hawi and others handled the logistics so that I could get from one place to another with the proper clothing and still have time to train and eat. It would have been nice to have more leisurely meals rather than eating in the car between events, but I wouldn't want to trade the experience for anything.

Receiving the Abebe Bikila Award, named after the great Ethiopian marathoner who won two Olympic titles, was the ultimate honor a marathoner can get. My doing so was a great example of Nelson Mandela's belief that sport unites us more than anything else, as I had escaped Eritrea because of conflict with Ethiopia. Also, it was awesome to get a surfboard with the marathon course map and my times and places on it from the New York Road Runners. It was an honor that so many people wanted to help celebrate my running career.

I was confident and excited when I finalized my goals for

the race. In descending order, they were to win, place in the top three, or place in the top ten. People might think I'm crazy, but I still thought that on a perfect day I could win the New York City Marathon at age forty-two. In terms of time, I knew I wasn't going to go out with a PR. I thought 2:11 would get me on the podium. (That turned out to be half true: Lelisa Desisa's 2:11:32 got him third place.) I also wanted to see how close I could get to 2:12:35, my time in my first marathon, run on the same course, fifteen years earlier.

My good friend and fellow Olympic Marathon medalist Deena Kastor told me, "I hope you finish high enough that you have to come out of retirement." I said, "No matter what the outcome, this is my last competitive marathon." After all the buildup, I was eager to get on with it.

BACK WHERE I BELONG

It was a beautiful day to run. The sky was overcast, with nice clouds. The temperature was 59 degrees when we started. The humidity was high, at 81 percent. I told myself to carry my fluid bottles longer than usual and take little sips rather than drink quickly and get right back to competing. I hoped to avoid the problems I had in Boston in 2015 and at the 2016 Olympics. The slower the pace, the easier it would be to implement this strategy.

I was in the zone and laser-focused once the race started. There were no thoughts like "The first 10K of my last marathon is behind me." The racing instincts I'd honed over the last twenty-seven years guided me. I stayed on the outside of the large lead pack to avoid getting tangled. I told myself to be patient and determined, that it was going to hurt at times, like it always did, and to bottle the energy of the supportive crowd for when I most needed it.

The early pace was very slow. The rest of the lead pack and I ran that first 10K of my last marathon in 32:00, around 2:15 marathon pace. The heavy favorites—two-time Boston winner Desisa; another Boston champ, Lemi Berhanu of Ethiopia; former world record holder Wilson Kipsang of Kenya; his countryman Geoffrey Kamworor, the world half marathon and cross-country champion—were watching each other, not the clock. New York would again be a tactical race, with a fast last 10K. This suited me perfectly. The pace picked up after 10K, but not dramatically. We passed halfway in 1:06:12.

At that point defending champ Ghirmay Ghebreslassie broke into a sprint on an uphill. Ghirmay had told me he was going to make that move. My 2002 self would have gone with him, and maybe we would have worked together to get away from the pack and then battle for the win. My 2017 self was literally twice as old as Ghirmay on race day. It would have been suicidal, if not impossible, to match his sprint. I needed to stay within myself.

Geoffrey Kamworor and a few others chased down Ghirmay but didn't continue the surge. I told myself I needed to catch them so that I could be in the lead pack on First Avenue. If my only goal had been to place in the top ten, I would have spread my energy more evenly and worked my way through the pack one by one in the later miles. But if I wanted to be on the podium I needed to be with the leaders on First Avenue, where there was likely to be another move. I made up a lot of ground—and used up a lot of energy—to rejoin the lead pack by the time we hit First Avenue in the 17th mile. Also, my right hamstring had started to tighten up.

What a treat it was to run down First Avenue in the pack of the New York City Marathon one last time! I couldn't contain my excitement. I gave thumbs-up and other small gestures to the crowds who were calling my name and otherwise making their usual energizing roar.

Ghirmay's sprint and the subsequent surges to catch him meant that we had slowed so that everyone could recover. The pace stayed easy on First Avenue. Too easy, in fact. Rule number one about pack racing is that once you initiate moves, you keep making them to increase the separation you've made over your pursuers. In my youth I would have surged at this point. While I wouldn't have had the turnover to go with the leaders if they'd thrown in a 4:30 mile, like I did in 2002, I wished someone had. The easy pace allowed the chase pack to catch up. Now the lead pack was twelve strong in the 19th mile, and it would be more difficult to meet my place goals.

BOWED BUT NOT BROKEN

My last time in the lead pack of a marathon ended soon after. Kamworor, the eventual winner, ran the 20th mile in 4:48. I simply lacked the turnover to keep up with that rapid increase in pace. I knew not to panic. If I kept running strong, some of the guys who covered the move would come back to me over the last 5K in Central Park.

At least that was what I told myself until disaster struck. Around mile 21, I started having heat hives, similar to what I'd experienced at the Rio Olympics. I felt the urge to vomit, and stopped to allow that to happen, but nothing came up. In all, I had five of these incidents over the final miles. They required me to slow to a jog or stop running altogether. Sometimes I vomited, sometimes I didn't. I think it was a combination of the hard move I'd made to catch the leaders before First Avenue and the high humidity.

Like I said in Chapter 22, I found that my body was more

affected by adversity once I was in my forties. As with previous incidents, this one was disappointing. I wasn't going to be able to finish fast and meet my top goals. Not because I'd made bad tactical decisions, not because I wasn't well prepared, just because my body wasn't cooperating.

At around mile 24, I heard that Shalane Flanagan had won, the first American woman to do so in forty years. It was so wonderful to hear that, especially because I was struggling and had already stopped three times. I got a spark of energy and did a little jump while raising my arms. Right after that I passed where Ryan Shay died during the 2008 Olympic Marathon Trials. I crossed myself and pointed to the sky in Ryan's memory.

The last two to three miles were my victory lap. I was still running as fast as I could, but now that my original goals were out of the question I switched my focus to enjoying the experience and the thrill of reaching the finish line. I didn't know what place I was in. At one point, I saw Ghirmay on the side of the road. I stopped briefly to hug him and encourage him to finish, but injury forced him to drop out. I was running alone and getting amazing individualized cheering from the crowd. I got very emotional feeling the love between us. I kept tapping my chest and pointing to fans and doing fist bumps to let them know how much I appreciated their support, on this day and throughout my career.

Reentering Central Park at Columbus Circle for the final 600 meters, I thought about what a wonderful journey my time as a marathoner had been. There was nobody behind me. I could have slowed and done more fist bumping, but I've always been a competitive guy. I wanted to finish as strongly as possible while still gesturing to the crowd to let them know I heard them. In whatever we do in life, it's important to finish strong. You can always rest when you're done. I took one last stride as a competitive marathoner and crossed the line in eleventh place in 2:15:29.

MISSION ACCOMPLISHED

When running is going well, you feel light. As soon as I finished that day, I felt like I weighed 200 pounds. I didn't know I was going to collapse right after the line, but I was definitely done. Fortunately somewhere I had the instinct to cover my head and protect it on the way down.

It was a scary moment. I had planned to celebrate finishing by reenacting my Rio Olympics push-ups. The NYRR had arranged for my parents, siblings, wife, daughters, and friends to be at the finish. I was going to embrace them all in gratitude for their support over the years. None of that was going to happen now. I didn't even have the energy to ask for a drink. I was totally depleted. Yordanos and others pulled me to my feet. Someone gave me a Snickers bar to get some sugar in my system. (I was looking forward to regular desserts in retirement, but not this soon!) I drank an electrolyte drink and some Generation UCAN. I felt revived enough to trot back down the finishing straight to thank the crowds one last time. I was more disoriented than I would have preferred for such a special moment, but that's the marathon. You do the best you can and don't let the setbacks defeat you.

One last marathon-as-metaphor-for-life observation: I went to bed that night with no regrets. I knew I had given it my all. I had measured myself, had paced myself, had reveled in the good times and persevered in the bad times. I had made the best of my God-given talents. I had done so on that day, and over the course of my marathon career. I had truly run to win.

THE RUN NEVER ENDS

Monday, November 6, 2017, was one of the most unusual mornings of my adult life. For the first time in twenty-seven years, I woke up not thinking about what I should do that day to prepare for my next race. It was a beautiful feeling.

Don't get me wrong: I loved competing against the world's best runners. Doing so made me a better person and gave me the opportunity to inspire others to run to win in their own way. But I truly believed I had tapped out my potential. I felt no lingering desire to have one more go at it, even though I didn't place as high or run as fast as I'd hoped in my final race. There was a sense of relief in not thinking, "What's next? How can I best get going on meeting that challenge?" I had always been looking ahead. Even after I won Boston, I immediately told Hawi, "Start talking to New York about this fall."

I had none of that urgency that morning. My thoughts about the future had to do with being more present for my family; spending more time with our daughters in daily activities; doing things that were off-limits as an elite marathoner, such as skiing, surfing, hiking, camping, and kicking a soccer ball in the backyard; and, yes, eating dessert or having a glass of wine without guilt.

That morning was also unusual physically. My stomach was still upset, and I had some blood in my stool. There was no doubt I'd left everything on the line in my final marathon. Otherwise, however, I was remarkably fresh. Thanks to the slow early pace and the great training I'd done, I felt more like I'd done a long tempo run than raced a marathon. My muscles weren't sore or tight. Even my old foot wound was fine. Usually I couldn't walk normally the day after a marathon, and was sore for four or five days. This time, I could do deep squats.

Three days after the race I did my first run as a retired pro. I felt great and wound up going six miles. This was sooner and farther than most of the initial runs after a marathon in my career.

I was so elated with the run that I shared an image from it on Instagram and my other social media feeds. Some people responded to the effect of, "Wait, I thought you were retired." Throughout that November and December I returned to near-daily running, sometimes going 10 miles, sometimes 6, and sometimes as far as 15. I kept sharing images and stats about the runs on social media, and people kept asking why I was running so much when I said I was retired.

Some world-class runners love racing but don't really enjoy training. That was never me. I always enjoyed training, both the daily pleasure of running and the process of building toward a meaningful goal. Being retired from professional racing doesn't mean being retired from being a runner. I simply love the feeling of running. I love being fit, healthy, and lean, and using the body that God gave me in the way it's meant to be used.

I love to run, and I hope to always be able to do it. I just don't want to race marathons. (I will admit I still have competitive thoughts. I'm an ambassador for the 2020 Olympic Marathon Trials in Atlanta. I find myself wondering how I'd stack up against the field at age forty-four.) I did twenty-six marathons over fifteen years, one for each mile of the race. I learned that the marathon can hate you or love you. It can make you go through misery or experience the greatest joy. I learned that no matter what happens, eventually you'll look back and think, "That was a beautiful thing. I'm glad I did it." That's how I feel about each of my marathons, and about my competitive career as a whole.

So I'm going to keep running. And I'm going to keep going to races and other running events. I'll run in some races, sometimes as a pacer to help others meet time goals, sometimes just to be part of the fun. I'll even hop in the occasional marathon and cover the course at training pace, to raise money and bring awareness to charities that are close to my heart, including, of course, the MEB Foundation. That's what I did at Boston 2018 for the Martin Richard Foundation, finishing in 3:00:13. At other races I'll be on the course or at the finish cheering. At all of them I'll share my love of running and the "run to win" message. I hope to see you out there.

Meb's Marathon Career at a Glance

MARATHON #	CITY / EVENT	DATE	PLACE	TIME
1	New York City	11/03/2002	9th	2:12:35
2	Chicago	10/12/2003	7th	2:10:03
3	Olympic Trials	02/07/2004	2nd	2:11:47
4	Athens Olympics	08/29/2004	2nd	2:11:29
5	New York City	11/07/2004	2nd	2:09:53
6	New York City	11/06/2005	3rd	2:09:56
7	Boston	04/17/2006	3rd	2:09:56
8	New York City	11/05/2006	20th	2:22:02
9	London	04/22/2007	Did Not Finish	
10	Olympic Trials	11/03/2007	8th	2:15:09
11	London	04/26/2009	9th	2:09:21
12	New York City	11/01/2009	1st	2:09:15
13	Boston	04/19/2010	5th	2:09:26
14	New York City	11/07/2010	6th	2:11:38
15	New York City	11/06/2011	6th	2:09:13
16	Olympic Trials	01/14/2012	1st	2:09:08
17	London Olympics	08/12/2012	4th	2:11:06
18	New York City	11/03/2013	23rd	2:23:47
19	Boston	04/21/2014	1st	2:08:37
20	New York City	11/02/2014	4th	2:13:18
21	Boston	04/19/2015	8th	2:12:42
22	New York City	11/01/2015	7th	2:13:32
23	Olympic Trials	02/13/2016	2nd	2:12:20
24	Rio Olympics	08/21/2016	33rd	2:16:46
25	Boston	04/17/2017	13th	2:17:00
26	New York City	11/05/2017	11th	2:15:29

ACKNOWLEDGMENTS

From Meb Keflezighi:

This book was made possible by many people who saw my marathon career span fifteen years. Thank you, Mark Weinstein, for sparking the concept and putting together the resources to make this book a reality. Usually, the opportunity to write a book comes only once in a lifetime. I'm grateful to Mark for giving me a third opportunity, and the second with the same team.

I would also like to thank Scott Douglas for his genuine love for the sport of running and for working so hard to make this book and *Meb for Mortals* a hit in the running scene. None of this would have been possible without the skilled guidance of my literary agent, D. J. Snell. Thank you for your hard work and for seeing the potential in my projects.

My brother and manager, Hawi, has been there for almost all of my marathon journeys. I appreciate your honest feedback on this journey.

My day-to-day reflector is my wife, Yordanos, who sees me go through these lessons and actions most of the time. Thank you for supporting me unconditionally as I learned these life and running lessons. I hope I have lived the lessons I have learned and help others use them in their daily runs, in their workplaces, and in their family time. Nothing is easy, but we learn to adapt.

Thanks to all the coaches who saw the potential in me to be a miler, and eventually a marathoner, and then as I attempted that challenge twenty-six times. Thanks to Coach Dick Lord, who planted the seed of running, and Coach Ed Ramos, who nurtured the seed with good water and advice. Thanks to Mike Anderson, a friend of the family, who said, "You will be a beautiful marathoner," before I knew the event was 26.2 miles long. Thanks to Ron Tabb, who saw the potential and who told me at age sixteen, "You have the potential to be a medalist," and warned me not to get distracted at UCLA and to look at the big picture.

Gail and Steve Van Camp cared for me genuinely and helped me come up with the "run to win" philosophy, which is discussed in this book and which fellow runners now have tattooed on their bodies and signed on their bibs.

Coach Bob Larsen told me to "show no mercy" before every race. You taught me to push hard every time to be the best I can be on that day but to never lose sight of the bigger goals.

Rich and Pat Levy are like my athletic parents. You were there when I needed someone to pace me or allow me to stay at your place so I didn't have to deal with traffic when I had a tempo run or long run scheduled. Also, thanks for being my cross-training partners. Both of you allowed me to put the miles on my ElliptiGO. Rich always told me, "You will know when it is not fun anymore. No one can tell you when to retire but yourself. The passion for competitiveness will die down."

To all my bike pacers: Thanks for sharing your time with me. You were the sounding board of my goals. Suresh and Gary, thank you for allowing me to stay at your places toward the end of my marathon career.

Thanks to all the physical therapists, doctors, and chiropractors who allowed my body to keep digging deeper to the finish line.

Thank you to all of the race organizers who helped me build my marathon career, especially the NYRR and the BAA.

Thank you to all my sponsors who have supported me so that I can be the best runner and ambassador possible. Special thanks to Skechers Performance and Dr. Lewis Maharam for allowing me to extend my marathon career when many thought it was over.

Thank you for this village that has raised me. Now I am part of the village that is raising our youth, our running community, and our elites.

From Scott Douglas:

Alyse Diamond, Meb Keflezighi, Hawi Keflezighi, and Stacey Cramp were paragons of patience while Meb and I wrote this book. Thanks to the book's original editor, Mark Weinstein, for his key role in bringing it to life.

PHOTOGRAPH INSERT CREDITS

Meb Keflezighi is one of the most accomplished runners in U.S. history. His victory at the 2014 Boston Marathon, one year after the bombings, made him the first American man to win the race in thirty-one years. He won the silver medal in the Olympic Marathon in 2004 and was fourth in the 2012 Olympic Marathon. During his long professional running career, Meb was also the 2009 New York City Marathon and 2012 Olympic Marathon Trials champion; won more than twenty national titles on the roads, track, and cross-country; and was an American record holder at 10,000 meters. He is a four-time U.S. Olympian (once at 10,000 meters, three in the marathon). He competed in the 2016 Olympic Marathon at age forty-one, making him the oldest Olympic marathoner in U.S. history. He remains the only runner to have won the Boston and New York City Marathons and an Olympic Marathon medal.

A native of Eritrea, Meb moved with his family to the United States in 1987 to escape the war then being waged between Eritrea and Ethiopia. He became a U.S. citizen in 1998, the same year he became a professional runner, and graduated from UCLA the following year. He is the founder of the MEB Foundation, which funds programs that promote fitness and other positive lifestyle choices for children. His life story was told in *Run to Overcome*. His second book, *Meb for Mortals*, made the *New York Times* best-seller list.

Meb retired from professional running after completing the 2017 New York City Marathon, his twenty-sixth race at the distance. He remains very active in the running community and elsewhere as a public speaker and brand ambassador. Meb lives in San Diego, California.

Scott Douglas is a contributing writer for *Runner's World*. He is the author or coauthor of several running books, including *Meb for Mortals*, *Running Is My Therapy*, and *Advanced Marathoning*. Scott lives in South Portland, Maine.

ALSO FROM MEB KEFLEZIGHI

Available in paperback and eBook
wherever books are sold.